With Love, Chaos & Rigatoni

JENNA HOLMES

WITH LOVE, CHAOS & RIGATONI

P MAMI'S GUIDE TO THE GOOD LIFE

CONTENTS

RISK
NOTHING
RECEIVE
NOTHING

CIAO!

Welcome to the colourful, chaotic world of P Mami and her many creative inspirations – plant design, indoor jungles, interior styling, sensory dining, community bonding, photography, art, simple pleasures, intuition, vibrant energy and following the sun. Whether you've picked up this book for some of my recipes, for travel tips to my favourite places, to get creatively inspired, or to better understand what makes me tick, you're in the right place. I'm going to share all of that with you – and more.

My family calls me Mays (after my middle name, May) and my inner circle knows me as JHo, a nickname created by my 10-year-old-self's adoration of Jennifer Lopez (aka JLo) and the perfect stage name for life, no? I'd prefer if you called me P Mami, as she is my professional alter ego and the creative maestro behind the magic in this book. That said, an old boss used to call me 'the friendly tornado' and a random lady on the street once called me and my dog Sprout 'walking lightbulbs', so I guess you can call me whatever you like – just keep it nice.

I wear a lot of blue, drink a criminal amount of San Pellegrino, break anything breakable I touch and want one day to live on a farm with 10 border collies and a pair of rescue llamas. If you get the opportunity to meet me in real life, you'll notice I have a loud voice, prefer being barefoot, wear paint-spattered clothes, cannot meditate or sit still past 12 minutes and love having at least eight different conversations at once. My gifts are my creative-styling eyes, my flavour-matching skills, how easily I work with and see colours, and my ability to make people feel comfortable, seen and inspired. On the flipside, I battle with the same insecurities we all do and have days where I'd rather stay in bed.

In 2021, I created P Mami Industries Pty Ltd, the mother company that houses Plant Mama, Pasta Club and Sheilas Club (currently on thoughtful pause). Plant Mama was my first fully-formed biz – a plant design studio I set up in Melbourne in 2017 that specialises in commercial and residential indoor jungles aka large-scale living art. In 2019, I added Pasta Club to the mix – a private sensory dining experience full of colour and organised chaos that encourages attendees to eat slow, savour flavours and create community connections. During the pandemic our business took off in unexpected ways, with our fresh merch and Pasta Club at Home packs regularly selling out. A bored entrepreneur with ADHD, a laptop and a broken ankle can do wonderful things during lockdown.

I guess you could call me the definition of self-made. There are no investors, rich parents, business loans, paid publicity or relevant uni degrees behind P Mami. Let me be your proof that it's possible to do anything with just an idea and a boatload of energy. The common thread across my endeavours is my injection of creative expression – I work tirelessly to bring *newness,* colour and warmth to everything I touch. In the beginning I did all the biz stuff too, but these days I focus my energy on being the creative director of a fast-expanding empire. Painting tablecloths, taking photos, designing tablescapes, making recipes, writing books, building jungles, creating playlists, meeting cool people and travelling are all in a day's work . . . but that doesn't mean the shit pies ever stop coming.

Although becoming P Mami has been a long, bumpy, overwhelming, passionate, soul-fulfilling and equally soul-destroying rollercoaster, it's one I freely chose to buy a ticket to and would do so again. Torching my stable teaching career to obtain a life of pleasure and freedom was the best decision I ever made. What I hope to show you through this book are the nine core principles I live by that guide all the decisions I make, big and small, to live the most creative and inspired life possible. Perspective, Passion, Pleasure, Personality, People, Power, Purpose, Places and Pain – with plenty of Pasta thrown in.

I hope you enjoy my unique perspective on the world. Whether that's the most delicious way to serve zucchini, why pain is a twisted gift, my literal view of life through film photos, or what happens when you act before you are ready. My life is not perfect, but it is authentic and focused on the simple wonders readily available to us all: shared meals, juicy peaches, a good book, great music and a nice beach to swim at. If you get nothing else from reading this, please learn how to relish *at least one* of these things. Because if not now, when?

With love, chaos and rigatoni,

YOUR CREATIVITY IS YOUR UNIQUE CONTRIBUTION TO THE WORLD.

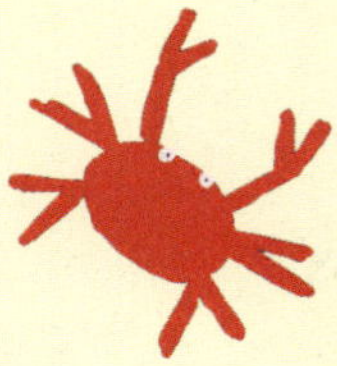

PROLOGUE: THIS TOO SHALL PASTA

Ever since I can remember, I've dreamed of ways to create a life that sees me getting paid for doing the things that I'm good at and that I love. Finally, after years of smashing against the world's ideas of 'success', I've made it!

Here I am, being paid to sunbake on a Greek island and write a book (this book!). Like always, I throw myself all in. To kick off our visit to Ikaria, my friend Steph and I spend the day at Seychelles Beach, the most *magnificent* place I have ever seen, but which demands grit and resilience to access. We clamber down a kilometre of near-vertical rockface to spend six blissful hours absorbing the Greek sun and sea, throwing back iced coffees before lunch and margaritas after. B-L-I-S-S.

Fast forward a mere nine hours and . . . life has turned to utter shit. Literally. Since coming off the beach, I've been shitting water non-stop. It's 2 am, I'm at the Airbnb, and though it's a stinking hot night, I'm shivering cold.

I drag myself across the ground toward the bathroom, desperate for a steaming hot shower. In the shower, I start vomiting. Now, I'm running between our two Airbnb toilets, vomiting in one, shitting water in the other. All I can think is what a luxury it is to be able to use different toilets . . . I know from past experience, being forced to combine the two generates its own death spiral. Gross.

Initially, I think it's heat stroke. Those eight hours lying in the sun chugging back Greek goodness with no water, and – hey presto! – heat stroke was almost guaranteed. But . . . no, no, no. As things go from bad to worse, it becomes clear that this is something else and very, VERY wrong. During a moment's rest, I google 'hospitals nearby'. I know my options are grim – I'm on an island that operates as if it's the 70s – but by some goddamn luck there's a 24/7 medical centre about five minutes away.

I drag my sorry arse over there, but as they have no pathology lab I'm transferred via ambulance to a hospital on the other side of the island and finally admitted at 6 am. I get every test under the sun: ultrasounds, X-rays, internal exams, bloods – the works. My pain continues, increasing until I am moaning and shivering uncontrollably. By 3 pm, having had no pain medication nor been given any indication of what's happening, I ask for the needles to be taken out so I can go home. Steph is due to fly back to New Zealand tomorrow and we need to exit our Airbnb.

'Oh no, you're not going anywhere,' says the doctor. 'You have appendicitis. Your appendix needs to be taken out. We are transferring you to another island.'

'Lady,' I say, 'I don't have appendicitis. I would know if I had, I'd be screaming in pain.'

'Well,' she replies, 'you're at the stage right before that, so there is no waiting – you must go. We've organised a medevac.'

Oh. My. Fucking. God. My literal *worst* nightmare: a small plane with me on it.

Luckily, the doctor on the plane clocks my panicked state and helps a sister out by flooding me with heavy-arse painkillers and playing the Beatles on his phone. God bless – I am certainly losing my mind by this point but, luckily, take a ride on codeine to get there. Twenty minutes later we land on the island of Samos and head straight to the hospital where I am placed in a wheelchair for about five hours until they can wangle me an emergency surgery slot.

When the time finally comes, still in agony, I'm given a surgical gown to change into and directed to a bed. I'm rolled into surgery and placed on a bench under a giant ring light. I can't understand what is being said to me, or around me. I know not a soul on this island and have nothing with me. Each minute, I become more terrified.

They begin slicing the front of my gown to expose my abdomen for cutting. I am really cold and begin shivering. I can feel blood dripping down the inside of my thigh. Oh great – day one of my period. Can this get *any* fucking worse?

The last thing I remember before passing out is the anaesthetist speaking to me. She can see the absolute terror in my eyes, the isolation and the confusion. And although I can't understand a word she says, she speaks calmly and reassuringly strokes my arm as she counts down from ten. *Deka, enéa, októ, eptá . . .*

chapter one

PERSPECTIVE

LIFE – IT'S HOW YOU FRAME IT

People seem to think I have some magic juice or secret sauce to share, but I'm not immune to life's shit times. What I have is a shift in perspective – knowing I have only one shot at this life, I wish to do it at 10,000,000 per cent. May I remind you we are floating on a ball in space so DO WHAT YOU WANT as it could all be over tomorrow. Say YES! to yourself every day that breath hits your lungs, knowing one day it won't. What separates most of us is how we choose to see life – how we shape the meaning of our problems and, as such, our existence. Perspective offers space to ease into what will unfold today and tomorrow. Lean in and see what magic yours can bring.

The sooner you realise no one's coming to save you, the sooner you can start looking after yourself.

RAINBOWS IN THE CLOUDS

None of us is able to outrun hard times in life forever. So, we must learn how to cultivate the skills to quickly call upon a state inside of us that can to locate the light when the dark rolls in and knocks on the front door. We must understand that the darkness is a necessary visitor on our porches, but we can dictate how far we let it into our house by controlling the only thing we can: our perspective.

It's 2 pm on a Sunday, and I am scream-crying on the phone to Dad. My newly repaired van, that I've just spent *thousands* on to fix, has broken down on the highway halfway between Melbourne and Byron. It is pelting rain, and I've only just managed to edge the van off the multiple-lane highway. Every time a road train roars past, my entire car shakes along with my heart and soul, and Sprout's too.

It is too unsafe to exit the car, so we remain inside while calling my insurer's roadside assistance. Because it's Sunday, no mechanics are open. The insurance company suggests towing me to the closest town to stay overnight and have someone look at the car in the morning. Good plan in theory . . . until we factor in Sprout and learn that no motel is willing to accommodate dogs. Finally, someone offers me mercy, but 'just for one night'. Normally I am able to locate a sunny disposition that insists 'This all has a purpose and will be FINE', but this time I take my emotionally exhausted self, Sprout and a McDonald's Happy Meal to bed.

Next day, the mechanic assessing my car says, 'It doesn't look good.' He tells me I'm going to have to leave the van behind and make other travel arrangements. After a quick panic attack, I rally. If I can just get to Sydney . . . I reach out to my Instagram community: *Anyone driving through Taree to Sydney??*

With zero replies, my situation is getting worse by the minute. I walk back to the motel for 10 am check-out and real panic sets in. I can't use public transport or hire a car because I have a dog. Asking a friend to make a six-hour round trip is too much to ask, even for me. I have already spent my emergency fund *fixing the van*, so I'm not in a position to throw cash at the solution, even if there was one.

I pack my bag and exit the motel and walk my sorry self and Sprout to the park behind. With nowhere else to go, here is where I plan to wait out the next few hours until the next van-intel update. We perch on a picnic bench and I grab my laptop. I have no game-plan, but I can't sit and do nothing – I just know I must take action. From nowhere, a thought begins to form. Although I have never sent out an 'email campaign' and don't know how to create one, this thought insists I should message my 2,000-plus waitlist subscribers. They have signed up through my website wanting to attend a public Pasta Club, but to date I haven't sent them anything. Now, this thought insists, is the moment.

I spend the next two hours YouTubing how to make an EDM and whip up an offer to my wait-listers to buy tickets to the first-ever public Pasta Club event. The work chews through my laptop power. As it nears five per cent, I stare at the 'send' button. Will this even work? I wonder. Have I just wasted two hours of energy on nothing? I bet no one will buy a ticket and this will be a joke in all their inboxes. As the battery drops to four per cent, I hit send and close the lid.

Like clockwork, my friend Sierra calls. I spend the next 10 minutes bawling my freaking eyes out and wiping snot all over my t-shirt.

'WHY DOES THIS SHIT KEEPING HAPPENING TO ME?!'

Of course, as best friends do, she talks me off the metaphorical cliff and helps me regulate, using four words we all need to hear: 'It will be okay', with a side of 'You're JHo! You're a warrior! Are you kidding me? This is SO MINOR compared with what you've handled before . . .' A much-needed rah-rah-rah that achieves its job *exactly*. While a strong self-perspective is helpful in life, having a solid one from the voices around you can be incredibly valuable when your own inner hype queen struggles to show up.

By the end of our conversation, I am fist-pumping. 'Yeah! Fuck yeah! You're right! I have literally dealt with so much worse. I've got this.'

We hang up the phone and I walk with Sprout toward the mechanic, preparing for my doom. As we walk, I open my Gmail, hoping against belief that maybe, just maybe, someone may have bought a ticket. OH. MY. MOSES. I literally have to SCROLL to get through the list of orders. We had sold out in 10 minutes, generating $8,000 worth of tickets.

My heart and soul burst and tears stream (again). Disbelief and gratitude spin through my body. I feel built up, ready to face whatever the mechanic has to say about my car.

As expected, the car is bad. He says they are unable to fix it, gifting me two enormous problems. First – getting the van somewhere else to be assessed; and second, getting my arse back to Sydney. Sprout and I have nowhere to stay and no

means of travel. Luckily, I can hand the car situation to Dad (he loves that stuff!). To solve problem number two, I head back to the park bench to ruminate.

Sitting there, I hear Maya Angelou whisper, 'Find a rainbow in the clouds' – and it jolts me back to my inner knowing. Somehow, I must find a way to be grateful for the clouds I am in. Especially after my email-campaign sell-out moment. So, I say thank you to the Universe. Thank you that I stayed safe, that Sprout is okay, that I had enough money to pay for last night's motel, for the plastic cheeseburger we ate, for a dad who's coming to save my car, for a sold-out first-ever email campaign. As I close out with, 'I trust this will all mean something,' BOOM, Ruby calls.

'Babe! I just spoke to my uncle Lawrence. His film shoot ended today and he's coming through Taree this afternoon! He can collect you and Sprout and has a spare room at his place in Sydney you can stay in while you make plans . . .'

CAN YOU FUCKING BELIEVE IT? Honestly . . . it took me a moment. I'd already met Lawrence several times with Ruby and we had a great connection – both across ADHD and creativity. There was no one *more perfect* who could have collected me that day.

Lawrence soon arrives with his film-mate Sunny (another legend!) and suggests we drop in to Seal Rocks on the way home for a sunset swim, snacks and doobie magic, knowing this elite combination will help recalibrate me after my emotional storm. Afterwards, we cruise down the highway listening to Coldplay super loud. I stare out the window, taking in all that's just happened. My rainbow arrived after all, and perspective was the thing that allowed it to spring so quickly into fruition.

A WIDER VIEW

I have made a conscious decision since my early 20s to locate and embrace the magical-big-shit possibilities constantly operating and buzzing around out there for all of us to grab onto. I've known deeply and intrinsically that every part of the process – good, bad or otherwise – has a specific purpose in contributing to the overall concept that is a human life. As I have been shown many times, although I can't control what's at play above me, I can control how I play the game. Hint: the easiest way is to trust the process, keep your head up for signs and move forward continuously with pitter-patter feet – always moving, always growing, always learning, always open.

I can say quite confidently that I am an optimist with realist tendencies. My mind and perspective have been trained to always find the positive and good in even the hardest of times (notice the word *trained*). My mum is a shining optimist and I believe that your family (like mine) will dictate which of the two you will become: a 'glass half full' or 'glass half empty' person. That's not to say that if you develop as one type you can't convert to the other, but you will need to train yourself against your normal thought pathways – a challenge worth accepting.

Rejection is always protection and setbacks are always setups.

Thankfully, Mum's life-coach teachings infiltrated my tweenie little brain and I began the art, very early on, of viewing every situation from above – eagle's-eye view, removed from the action – so I can see constructively *why* each person may have behaved the way they did, or said the things they said. This basis of believing in GEWD THANGS ONLY has been built by my parents and the gazillion books I've spent almost a quarter of a century absorbing into my curious little noggin.

One thing I swiftly learned is that you can bet your sorry arse life will simultaneously build you up as it beats you down. No one is exempt from this. What separates certain people from others, however, is our ability to continue once the beating has subsided, knowing that since we're unable to avoid pain, we might as well adjust how we're viewing it. I look at pain as being a crucial part of the process of living, rather than a personal attack on my existence. Rejection is always protection and setbacks are always setups . . . but more on that in Chapter 9, where we focus on the Pain Principle.

Principle 1, Perspective, has been my refuge in life, allowing me to lean in with blind faith at times of trial. I am not part of any organised religious group yet I strongly believe there's something out there guiding me and I have tangible proof of this, as you shall read about shortly. For me, spirituality is a belief that something greater – what I call the Universe – is operating with you to co-create your life. I see this as an inward journey that involves a search for meaning and purpose and which comes from a place of self-awareness. To me, spirituality is *being*, religion is *believing* – and both exist, together and separately.

While all that might sound a bit woo-woo, it would be impossible for you to read parts of my story without considering how perspective and my spiritual practices have contributed to my being where I am today, way beyond starting P Mami Industries. Luckily, as each year passes, I gather more people in my orbit who talk the same talk, walk the same walk and connect with me over our shared understanding of this greater power. This has given me courage to share my wild stories and forgo the bullshit of worrying about what people think, in order to serve and help others where possible.

I don't need to repeat that 'no two journeys are the same' yadda yadda, but what I can say is that I learned everything I know from others deciding to open their vaults to me. Just as others have shared with me their struggles and the approaches that helped them, I pay it forward by opening my own vault to expose the chaotic but wonderful things that reside inside. Any successful person in life or work will tell you that difficulties are always part of the parcel and it's the opportunities we seek in the middle of the storm that add a resilience layer against the next one. This perspective pushes me every day to consider how I can do a little bit better. How *we can all* do a little bit better.

NO TV FOR YOU

We start this story in 1999. It's the end of December, just after Christmas, at my family home in Toowoomba, Queensland. We have a few more weeks left of summer school holidays after which I'm going to a new primary school and my brother will head off to high school. As a way to 'shake up the system' and ensure that Cameron and I do not head down the 'digitally distracted teenager' route, my parents have just laid out a new family rule. (Typically, we'd get served these a few times a year over family dinner. Never a conversation up for debate, rather an instruction for a new way of living.)

'We have decided that when school goes back you're only allowed to watch one hour of television a day on weekdays. You can choose your show and either watch it before school or when you get home, or even after dinner. You get one hour, no more. Instead of TV, you can go play outside, or do your homework. Watch as much television as you want for the rest of the holidays, but when school goes back it's one show. Choose wisely.'

Obviously, at this point in life, we were *not* chill about our television rights being revoked! *Are you kidding me?* Cam and I had a deep love–hate sibling relationship growing up, so it was rare for us to work together, but on this we agreed. We *totally* lost it at Mum and Dad. TV WAS LIFE. IT WAS EVERYTHING. I mean, we were tweens in a small town just before the year 2000. While the internet had arrived on a CD (shocking quality but nonetheless revolutionary), TV still reigned supreme.

As we entered those final three weeks of fulltime screen bingeing, I found myself watching random shows at irregular times – hello, lunchtime television. Choosing my one show was the biggest decision of my life, so I was dedicated to absorbing all my options so I could make an informed and satisfying decision that future me would be stoked with.

I distinctly remember flicking the channel and seeing John Travolta, who I recognised from *Grease*, and some smiling woman interviewing him. I was instantly drawn to their 'friend chemistry' (non-sexual, buzzy energy between people) and found their conversation interesting, thoughtful and full of laughter. As the credits rolled – *The Oprah Winfrey Show* – I remember an unexplained lightness in the air. This energy drew me back the following day.

By the time the holidays were up, I'd seen almost a dozen *Oprah* episodes covering an array of often-hilarious topics like, 'What's your beauty age?' and 'Responsible choices with Gary Zukav'. Half of it I didn't fully understand, but

I was nonetheless under the show's spell. I had fallen into a little world where the adult conversations happening in front of me were sparking my interest – I wanted to hear it ALL.

I was not only gifted some joyful viewership, but also some incredibly shocking and painfully real stories. I remember a dad from Connecticut who had lost his two daughters and wife after a couple of guys saw them all at the local supermarket one morning. The guys followed them to the family home and broke into the house. They separated the women, tied them up, sodomised, abused and tortured them, then burnt the house down. The dad was able to escape through the basement, but not before he'd had to endure hearing his girls suffer. It's the type of story that stays with you forever.

On *The Oprah Winfrey Show*, these types of stories were featured every few days as the topics were so vast. I witnessed some super tough and confronting stories that are normally sheltered from children's eyes. They opened my consciousness to the extreme levels of the human experience and the realisation that not everything is wrapped in cotton wool or easy. *Some really terrible things happen to really great people.* So, be great and be good, but let it be known that terrible things can come just because they do. That's why I always say, enjoy the sun when it's shining, because at some point, it won't.

D-Day finally came. School was tomorrow and our new television-free life was about to begin. I had considered my options long and hard. While it would be incredibly traumatic to let go of watching *Arthur*, *The Secret World of Alex Mack* and several iconic ABC after-school shows, my choice was made.

The conversation around the dinner table was of epic *Survivor* tribal-council magnitude. My turn finally came around and without hesitation, I spoke. 'Oprah.'

Mum was proud, Dad was confused and Cameron thought I had just executed the dumbest decision in human history.

Of course, every important journey encounters roadblocks and mine came in the form of the family VCR machine. *Oprah* aired during school hours, so if I wanted to watch it after school then I would have to record it every day. The night before school went back, I spent hours working my little fingers across the world's most complicated recording service and eventually managed to set my first timer. The next day I was delighted to return home from school and find I'd successfully taped the show, minus a few hiccups. Thus began a daily routine that would continue for the next eight years, until I finished high school.

THE THING ABOUT OPRAH

I only recently found the space to consider what *exactly* pulled my teenage self toward Oprah. During an interview for the ABC podcast *Days Like These*, I was asked to deconstruct my calling to the show and why I read her magazine and all the books she recommended. This was quite unusual for a young teen, my interviewer observed. While I responded lightly at the time, the question became ever-present in my brain.

Now, with a decent amount of reflection and gelato-eating time, I realise quite clearly that there is a definite correlation between me starting to watch *The Oprah Winfrey Show* and my feelings of disconnection during that time. Against the terror of starting a new school at 10 years old and the isolation of high school that followed, I found solace in my daily episode of meaningful conversations and lessons. Looking back, up until the age of 18, my days felt drained of energy, only refilled by my 4 pm hour with Lady O.

When casting my mind back to little J in her school uniform watching those episodes on the couch, it is incredibly clear that she was seeking something deeper. Looking for a connection, she was fascinated to hear stories about the human experience and receiving huge worldly concepts, spiritual practices and life lessons during the most brain-sponge and info-absorbent years. I only finished my viewership aged 21, when the show ended in 2011. The connection and relationship between myself and Oprah was not one of a celebrity crush, rather a uniquely powerful teacher–student connection and I felt deeply thankful to be a part of her classroom 16,000 kilometres away in Chicago.

Fast forward to October 2008. I am 18 years old and working, during my gap year before university, at the local gym. This particular day I had a 5 am shift which allowed me to get home for lunchtime *Oprah* and that day's feature, *The Secret* by Rhonda Byrne. Byrne's book about the 'law of attraction' explores the concept that the energy and thoughts you project into the world determine what gets returned to you and how this principle helps you manifest your deepest desires.

Several times over the episode, Byrne made it *very* clear that to achieve one's dreams there must be action – you must 'put in the work'. You cannot just say, 'I want a million dollars,' and BAM! there it is in your account. You must envision what you want, believe you can get it, write it down, take actionable steps toward achieving it, and continue to visualise and believe you will get it. The episode discussed creating a 'vision board' – finding and pasting images of your desires onto an artboard to create a constant visual reference of the things you want to manifest. Ideally, you place it somewhere in your home where you can see it all the time, to be reminded of your tangible goals and the actionable steps you need to take to achieve them.

At the end of the episode, Oprah's call to action was for everyone to go and begin making their vision board – you could see she was deeeeeply passionate about this law-of-attraction business. I felt like she was talking to me directly through the TV, saying, 'Jenna, go get in your car and get to Officeworks now!'

So, I did. That very afternoon I acquired a 40 cm x 50 cm canvas board and several glue sticks and sped home to begin. I pondered over my images/visuals for about an hour. What do I want? What images will best represent this? I wrote a little list, used Google to locate matching images, placed them all on a Word doc and colour-printed it on our crappy home printer. I cut out each image then glued them all to my canvas, making sure I left gaps so I could add stuff later if new thoughts came to mind. I won't share everything on the canvas 'cause some of that shit's private, but here's a little sneak peek:

MY VISION BOARD

- A quote from Oprah: 'There is no such thing as luck, just preparation meeting opportunity.'
- Celine Dion's legs
- a Range Rover
- the word 'chutzpah'
- a dog and some llamas
- a collage of me + Oprah + salad bowl, signifying: I'll have lunch with Oprah one day.

Once completed, my vision board found a home on the wall across from my bed, so I saw it every day when I woke up and right before I went to sleep. I knew the key was to create a daily *subtle reminder* that could sink in over time. I was not dreaming every night of my legs transforming into Celine's or visualising getting 'chutzpah' tattooed on my forehead; rather, getting my subconscious to remember the larger goals at play. My twice-daily visual alarm reminded me of the manifestation required and I held a sound belief that these things would happen, because – how could they not?

I WANT JENNA TO MEET OPRAH

We fast forward again, this time to 2010, and Oprah has announced she will be ending her show the following year. Mum and I are talking about how I've always dreamed of attending one of her live tapings and she says, super flippantly, 'Well, if we ever get tickets to a show then I will take you. You can either have a 21st birthday party or I'll take you to America to see Oprah.'

SORRY WHAT? WOT? WAT?

Okay, well *this* is stunning, I thought, but also extremely impossible. I had literally been applying for tickets since I could remember, with no luck. Even people who *lived* in America had been unable to get tickets for decades so . . . what were my chances? Turns out, pretty high. Something opened up and we randomly got tickets! Maybe that vision board was beginning to work.

We flew to a special taping in LA. I was there in the live audience to watch Oprah in action. I was buzzing! And yet . . . When she walked out on stage I was hit with a very clear, pure message. As Oprah entered the room and every human in it jumped up in excitement with roars of clapping, a little voice said to me, 'Oh yes, so this is nice, but don't worry, you'll meet her another time. Enjoy this, but there is more to come. Better things!'

I mean, what?! This was like THE most exciting thing that had *ever* happened to me. But that whisper told me something very clear. This was only the beginning.

Months later, I was woken to 20-plus messages on my phone from multiple people. My gut dropped – *uh-oh! What's the bad news?* Nothing, it was GREAT! Oprah had announced that as a thrilling climax to her final season she would take the entire audience to Australia where she would film not one, but TWO live shows 'Down Under'. In that moment, I *knew* this was it – what my whisper had been about. I jumped on to Oprah.com for details and found a little box headlined, 'Aussie Ultimate Viewers – Write to us!' requesting Australian fans to send in a story about their experience for a chance to win seats.

Write in? I thought, *Puuuuhhhhhhhhleeeassse*. Like every other man and his dog? No, no, no! I must STAND OUT to be seen. I must do something different and unique. This deserves to be a cinematic experience or a feature film! If there was ever a time to Not-Be-Boring then THIS WAS IT! I do not think I have ever moved faster in my life as I worked toward making my pitch video. Luckily,

I was studying 'Documentary' as a uni subject, so I took those lessons (and the uni camera) and worked on forming a short five-minute video.

First, I explained the hugely positive impact that *The Oprah Winfrey Show* had had on my life. Then, I interviewed my friends and family and recorded them talking about who I was as a person because of the show (LOL!). Still, I knew I needed something 'high value' to increase my chances of getting seen, like a community petition, but in another form . . .

I got Dad to help me get a sign made up. On a large hard board we printed: I WANT JENNA TO MEET OPRAH!! with two smiley faces on the end, 'cause . . . duh, why not? And then I took that fucking sign with me EVERYWHERE. In Brisbane I snapped over 370 photos of different people holding it. I took it in my luggage to Perth for University Sports Games and got several dozen more photos there. I carried it to work and hustled gym members for a picture. Friends brought siblings and friends of friends to get a photo with the sign. In just a few short weeks I collected over 500 photo 'signatures'.

Now for the finishing touch: a song. Given my ABBA obsession, there was only one choice. 'Take A Chance on Me' played while images of hundreds of random people holding my Oprah sign flashed across the screen. I submitted the video and within a week or so the Oprah team made contact and were organising to talk to my mum about me and Oprah and a bunch of other things. It was all very exciting but then, after a few weeks of chatty emails back and forth, they went dead silent. No communication, no response, no nothing. As you can imagine, I was devastated. I didn't know what to do.

Soon after this, the tickets for the live show went up with millions of people entering the ballot. I was furious as I saw people who didn't even watch the show wave around their confirmation emails across Facebook. We waited and waited, but no tickets for us. My dream was shattered.

Eventually came the day when the US audience and Oprah arrived in Australia. My family were holidaying on the Sunshine Coast and Oprah was being broadcast everywhere, on every news channel. There was no way to miss the flood of updates on Oprah's every move, each another sharp reminder of my failed pitch. Seeing my desperate sadness and disappointment, Mum invited me for a coffee downstairs at the café.

This next particular part of the story will go down in history as one of the most powerful and conscious moments I have ever experienced and sometimes it still gives me shivers. To be honest, when I look back and reflect, it's pretty clear that this was the beginning of my journey and trust in the spiritual realm.

We sat down and ordered our coffees, initially engaging in light chat, both knowing that a more serious conversation would soon follow – something I had learned to expect from my wisdom-filled coffee chats with Mum. Her perfectly timed speech went something like this:

> Mays, I just want to remind you that you made the most amazing video. It was magnificent. It's just that someone else needs that ticket and experience in this moment, so it's just not for you at this time. This does not take away from your hard work and great idea - it was amazing! You should be so proud. Dad and I are so proud.
>
> Yes, it's going to be hard to see everyone going to the shows and Oprah all over Australia, but you must remember this: You made an intention, showed up and worked really hard toward it, gave it your best try, and now . . . it's time to let it go.
>
> Your time will come, don't worry. I promise another opportunity will be offered to you. Just let the disappointment float off your shoulders and be content with what you gave to this. The Universe always remembers what you did and where you live, so it will happen another time. Let it go.

Now I can say, with all the fibres in my being, that in that moment, for the first time in my entire life, I *physically* experienced what it feels like to be released from something. I literally saw my sadness, attachment and disappointment rise to the top of my shoulders and, on a set of angel-like wings, float away. I was left completely clear and at peace. I recognised my efforts toward trying to achieve my goal and accepted that this time around it wasn't for me. There was not one thing left in me that could now be triggered by the words, 'Oprah Down Under'. It was a truly miraculous feeling.

Shortly after, we finished our coffees and headed back to the apartment. As I walked through the door, I heard my phone ringing. I scrambled to find it among my bed covers and answered the random number. A voice with an upbeat, friendly American accent said, 'Hi Jenna, it's Amanda calling from *The Oprah Winfrey Show.*'

This. Cannot. Be. REAL! My stomach flipped, I started sweating and while on the phone, ran out to the living room. Using my best charades skills, I somehow managed to communicate to my family that OPRAH'S PEOPLE ARE ON THE

PHONE! Everyone was quietly beating lounge pillows and jumping up and down like maniacs. If only I'd had the camera rolling!

Amanda had called to offer me tickets to a taping of the show. While delighted, I was also stuck – I had tickets to Bon Jovi that night in Brisbane, I explained, and Oprah was in Sydney. 'That's fine,' Amanda replied. 'Let's get you on the morning taping so you can go to both Oprah and Bon Jovi – how fun!' After running through more details, she finally hung up, only to call back moments later. 'Oh,' she said, 'I just wanted to say, it's going to be hot, so bring some powder for your face in case you get sweaty.'

We arrived at the Sydney Opera House for the live show and were greeted by the longest line we had ever witnessed in our entire lives. After waiting for about 45 minutes, we heard a voice over the loudspeaker. 'If you have a green wristband, then please head to the front gate now.'

We looked down – green wristbands! No one else around us had them, so lucky us, we jumped forward. As soon as we reached the front, we were assigned a lovely lady who walked us to our seats. We walked further and further along the pathway, until we finally arrived at two seats in the front row, right next to the stairs, marked by a sign that read: 'Holmes x 2'.

Over the next hour or so as the rest of the audience filled the seats, Mum and I were randomly approached by various members of Oprah's team. Many mentioned my submission video – how they'd watched it the previous night at a staff meeting and were elated to see that someone my age, in Australia, was so engaged with their content and conversations.

The show started and was everything I had expected – and more. Finally, my moment! Watching Oprah in front-row seats, in the forecourt of the Opera House, Sydney Harbour sparkling as a backdrop. I would remember this morning forever. We were nearing the end of the show with only one more segment to go and during the break I noticed a cameraman bring Oprah a giant white card. She held it against her chest so we couldn't see what was written on it.

Mum heard the cameraman say, 'She's the one in the colourful shoes and red dress, front row.' At that exact moment, I saw Oprah look down at my shoes, then back at me, wink and smile. Then, with no further warning, my submission video got blasted on the three screens behind her. In slow motion, I saw my head pop up across the giant screens.

'Hi! I'm Jenna from Australia.'

Multiple hands tapped and grabbed me from behind. 'That's you! That's you!'

After what felt like five seconds, the video ended and Oprah asked me to stand up in front of the 12,000-strong crowd. She then sang-yelled in her classic Oprah voice, 'Well, Jenna, I have a sign for YOOOUUUUUU,' and flipped over an *exact replica* (font, exclamation marks, smiley faces) of *my* sign, except it read: 'I WANT JENNA TO MEET BON JOVI!!'

And, BOOM! Bon Jovi and his band mates came out on stage. By this moment, I was well and truly having what Oprah calls an 'out of body' experience – where you are so present in the moment you are unable to recall it. That is *exactly* what this was. Beyond. Truly beyond.

Bon Jovi sang my two favourite songs while the cameraman filmed my reaction. Although Mum could see him, she assumed they'd cut her out, so she was busting some hardcore dance moves (if you can somehow get your eyes on that *Oprah* clip, it's easily the greatest scene of them all!). After Bon Jovi finished, Oprah asked me up on stage to meet Jon. As I walked up, I could see him and his hair walking toward me in slow motion. I *literally* went weak at my knees when he came up to hug me. *WHAT IS HAPPENING HERE? WHAT IS THIS? THIS IS NOT REAL!*

The show ended and people fled to miss the traffic. I was still in shock at what had just unfolded, when a producer of the show approached and asked Mum and me to come backstage to sign a release form. We headed into Oprah's green room which, as you can imagine, was a stunningly beautiful space set out with comfy couches, flowers and lots of food. By now I was feeling elated, but exhausted and ready to go (I had to get to Brisbane for Bon Jovi's concert, remember!), so I was a little deflated when, instead of quickly grabbing my signature, the staff members directed us to grab some refreshments and take a seat.

My feelings changed when, moments later, in casual clothes and flat shoes, Oprah glided on in – alone, no team. As she proceeded to get some food, she oh-so-casually said, 'Hi, Jenna. How wild was that, huh?' then walked over to my mum and me. Over what felt like two hours (but was more like 15 minutes), I sat on the couch, casually talking to Oprah about my life and hers, eating salad.

Do you recognise this image? I sure did: Me + salad bowl + Oprah – the exact scene from my vision board. I had set an intention, visualised what I wanted, given *everything* I had to it, then let go of the outcome. Hey presto – IT FUCKING WORKED!

Soon after, Oprah's team arrived and she was rushed off to the next engagement, but not before I shared a letter I wrote to her, started by my 13-year-old self and finished by my 20-year-old self, thanking her for the enormous impact her teachings had gifted me. It acknowledged that had she not so authentically shared herself I would not have been encouraged to do the same. My nine-, 13-, 21-, 33-, 57- and 88-year-old selves will be eternally grateful to have been one of her students because, no doubt, her impact has been monumental. As we left, the team gave us the 'Bon Jovi' sign. Both it and my original vision board have pride of place in my childhood bedroom to this day.

The lesson from this story has shaped my entire life, as I was able to see the power of manifestation at work in real life through such a big-impact event – and this is how most of my life seems to be, if I am honest. Loud lessons, big thoughts. In a way, I was at the right time and age to learn such a lesson, as if the Universe was graduating me from high school to UNIVERS-ity and I was getting a very loud crash course in the basics. But, with OPRAH WINFREY. Far-fucking-out, huh? This has led me to establish a foundational underpinning to my days, which is to:

- Visualise where I want to go.
- Take the necessary steps forward and stay focused.
- Let go of controlling the journey and the outcome.
- Arrive where I am meant to be.
- Take any roadblock or redirection as a gift.

There is a cycle and a process to achieving your dreams and your goals, all of them being entirely possible if you are: first, able to distinguish exactly what you want; and second, willing to accept that roadblocks along the way are inevitable, so let go, but never give up. The Universe won't grant your desires if it can't hear you. It does not know how to decipher rambling Randall! It needs clear intentions, spoken concisely and directly – and wants to know what you are bringing to the table so it doesn't get the raw end of the deal, and *fair enough* I say. The Universe has a large clientele to serve.

If you follow this practice, you'll go to work on your intentions and feel that nothing is happening for a while – that's the Universe testing whether you're going to give up or stay focused. You see, that's the trick it plays, to see *how badly* you want this thing. Take heart, as the blessed thing always follows the worst thing. Once the Universe sees you doing the hard work, showing up every day and sticking to the deal you made, then *just watch* and see what shows up. Cross my heart and hope to die. Socks will be knocked off.

One tip though, we tend to want to control the things we do not trust, right? So . . . the biggest part of this story is the letting go part, okay? You must trust that whatever the outcome, the Universe is always working for your growth, not against it.

The newest version of my vision board is a lunch bowl that sits next to Cate Blanchett and Sarah Paulson: the ultimate P Club pairing. Can someone out there make it happen, please? Or . . . maybe, I just can. Scratch that – not maybe. Can. Will. Trust.

EVERYTHING
PASSES.

TRUST IN THE UNIVERSE – AND IN YOURSELF

Whether I became more spiritually aware because of Oprah, or I was attracted to Oprah because I was already searching, I'll never know, but one thing's for sure – around the time I started watching Lady O, I also began a dedicated search to understand myself, the Universe and my place in it. This has been cultivated through four key things: my mum, Oprah, books and my curious personality. Over what feels like millions of hours of reading and contemplating the spiritual rah-rah, I have absorbed a range of teachings that help me deal in times of crisis.

The most important thing I have learned is that regardless of the strength of your family and friend relationships, the most consistent, available, everlasting and powerful relationship is the one you have with yourself. It took me a while to learn to trust my inner self, but it's been well worth it. Searching for her, finding her and listening to her has taught me many things as she's rather chatty, you best believe!

The biggest hunky lesson of all is this: It comes down to how you frame things. You can't change what happens to you – not the hand you're dealt, the star you were born under and most especially, not the rain once you've finally hung out your laundry (a once-in-a-blue-moon thing for me). Your perspective and your awareness of e.v.e.r.y.t.h.i.n.g you experience is the *only* thing you can control.

Before you freak out too much, let me quickly explain where I sit on the 'woo-woo' spectrum, as this may help my realist readers to relax a little. I am *yet* to do the following: own a vast variety of crystals, have a yoni massage, try Ayahuasca, enjoy yoga, put my period blood on my plants, sing to the moon naked, or invest in drinking essential oils to clear my sacral chakra. But, I *have* studied level-one reiki, micro-dosed psilocybin, participated in breathwork and inner-child workshops, had energy healing and seen many lightworkers across a range of spiritual practices.

It's also worth mentioning that both my parents are hard-working, disciplined folk who follow Christian teachings. I'm glad to have inherited the former, but I've gone my own way on the latter. When I had the conversation with Mum about unsubscribing from our family's religion it was scary as hell. But, there

Some days, I fully desire to blow the Universe up. I have felt betrayed, alone, violated and really angry.

was also respect. Mum has always encouraged my search for greater meaning, even paying me $10 for every self-help/spiritual book I read growing up. From these humble beginnings and many life lessons since, I have learned these things . . .

Your soul is undertaking a journey and requires guidance as it moves forward: a helping hand, a gentle tap on the shoulder, or a nudge redirecting you to somewhere else. As you follow your own inner knowing and energy radar, you work in conjunction with the Universe. To accept this partnership and join forces is the most effective relationship possible. When friends do not answer the phone and family feels far away, the Universe is *always* there. When my books do not have the answers and empowering YouTube speeches from David Foster Wallace have not done their hype job, the Universe is still there. When I am crying at 3 am and overwhelmed by anxiety, huge business things and stress, it's there – reminding me of who I am and *what this will teach me*.

Don't get me wrong, it ain't all sunshine and daisies with this partnership. Some days, I fully desire to blow the Universe up. I have felt betrayed, alone, violated and really angry. Pain needs a perpetrator and sometimes the Universe is that – because sadly, pain is an integral part of the human experience; it's how we grow, become better and learn to react differently. Many times, I have sworn off the Universe as I rail against its heavy-hitting lessons, only to realise later that I had been operating in misalignment with myself. While the Universe was giving me the lessons, I was definitely creating the issues by not following my gut and the both gentle and not-so gentle signs it was giving me. The Universe does not ever say 'no' to you. It's either 'not yet', 'yes' or 'something better'.

You might know your Universe and have a strong connection to it, or maybe you're considering it for the first time and want to dip your toe in. It's okay, we can go slow; we don't need to try and boil the ocean here. I can guarantee that the sooner you start opening yourself up to receiving the messages and signals the Universe is trying to send to you, both physically and mentally, the quicker you will locate the (correct) path that's been yelling, 'COME OVER HERE AND JOIN US!'

You will already have seen your Universe operating its magic, but maybe you didn't know what it was. If something feels coincidental, then that's your first sign. By opening your mind juuuust a little, you can cultivate and access your internal 24/7 HELP centre forever. And, it's free!

I know for some of you it feels weird and freaky and very new to consider this all, especially so quickly into the book but hey, it's the foundation of P Mami – so if we're gonna get to know each other, we gotta do it right. This is *the thing* I've relied on behind the scenes the entire time. Denying its impact would be incredibly rude and also . . . if you're not slightly uncomfortable at one point during this read, then my teaching is not good enough.

Personally, I believe your journey blueprint is inked the day you are born and you're unable to dictate beyond it at the larger scale. Yes, your thoughts create your reality and you can choose to change your direction in life by your own will; however, what I have found is that no matter how hard I try to redirect a teaching or (ideally) just ignore it completely, I will still be pressed to face it and learn from it. Until I absorb the message, it will get louder and louder – what you resist, persists. Through life there is always a spiritual lesson or growth experience unfolding, regardless of whether you're in your safe hometown or on holidays in the south of Sardinia.

The Universe can and will screw with you anywhere and everywhere and, in a lot of cases, at the most stressful times and places. What it's doing in these instances is testing you: how you react, what you say to others and yourself, how you bring in past teachings, your reflection, your intention and then what you change. I have noticed that the solutions to my problems are implemented with more clarity, thought and intention when I work my spiritual practices alongside my reliance on the Universe and my intuition to help guide me in deciding the best next move to take.

There are always signs available; however, it is impossible to see them if you are not open to receiving them. Eventually, after much trial and error, I have reached the point I'm at now, where hints, messages, subtle energy changes and gut feelings are available to me 24/7, pushing me toward *what feels right*. While I will never be free from making mistakes or incorrect decisions, at least my rate of success is higher now, as I look for the signs while trusting my intuition to do the work. Always.

Do not let the fear of this enormously powerful relationship scare you off forming a deep connection with it, as it has the capacity to transform your life for the better. At least, that's what's worked for me. And, as you'll read in the rest of this book, it is constantly at play, making our whole existence truly 'n' wildly 'n' deeply remarkable. You'll notice through all my crazy stories, something bigger at play. It's undeniable. What other explanation is there? The sooner you trust that your life is unfolding as it's meant to, the sooner you will stop wasting useless energy on worrying about whether things will all work out or not. In the end, they *always* do.

As I rotate the sun with gratitude, aware of the privilege of having lived another year, I reconfirm three things that are the forever truth:

- *Tutto passa*: everything passes
- *Meglio soli che male accompagnati*: better alone than in bad company
- *Dolce far niente*: sweetness in the art of doing nothing.

That all said, I absolutely acknowledge the work it takes to maintain an optimistic outlook. It took me a while to overcome little J's conditioning and natural temperament and cultivate a more positive way of talking to myself. Stemming from my own lack of self-love, my childhood instinct was to think of myself as 'too much' or doing something wrong. I have the same anxieties as you, often waiting for everything to explode, but I've worked hard to redirect my thinking in those moments. What if it turns out *better* than I imagine? This is only possible because I have put the man hours into rewiring how I make sense of things. My perspective was not built in a day.

PRINCIPLE 1

Perspective

It is impossible to learn nothing from something if you're willing to change your perspective. You decide what becomes wasteful or useful.

Keep one eye fixed on your dreams. You will receive help toward what you want when you know what you want.

The way you view yourself has a powerful impact on your life. Make you a priority and keep evolving.

Ask yourself

What is your 'inner company' motto? (Hint, mine is: I am capable of anything and have whatever I need inside of me.)

When have you felt something greater assisting you in life?

Does finding the good in things come naturally to you, and if not, how might you switch your perspective?

Do you know what you want and have you made it clear to yourself and others?

Are you the driver or the passenger in your life?

chapter two

PASSION

FOLLOW YOUR CURIOSITY

Passion is the spark we need to begin anything warm and special. It arouses great enthusiasm; a powerful feeling that, at times, feels uncomfortable and uncontrollable. Plant Mama and Pasta Mama are two big things that arouse my passion, but I'd be lying if I didn't admit that at least once a week I vow to sell everything P Mami-related and go milk goats in Sardinia. I stay because the fulfilment, alignment and sense of self that arise from passion's driving force is the fuel that feeds my inner fire. If you're wondering how to locate your passion, then let me show you what helped me. It's not about turning your passion into your work, or even making money from it, but about finding what tickles your curiosity and pursuing that.

The only way
to really know
passion is to
throw ourselves
all in and
experience it
in its entirety.

LOOKING FOR TURTLES

Starting out on your passion journey may be one of the hardest steps you take. In the beginning, it's just you and your dreams. Sometimes, not even that. It could just be an inkling, a curiosity. But if you fan that spark, a tiny flicker may ignite.

It is 2019. He is tall and skinny, maybe late teens or early twenties, and wearing baggy jeans and an oversized shirt, scruffy hair – the classic artist look. All weekend, as I've been running in and out of my studio in Collingwood, I've seen him standing out front of the gallery next door, asking passers-by to come in and see his work. While Melbourne folk are uber supportive of the creative arts, they can sometimes be quite rude. Although just about everyone has fobbed him off, me included, it hasn't deterred him. He just keeps asking.

By Sunday, it feels like I've been out all weekend. I come home tired and see art-guy still gatekeeping the gallery. This guy does not give up! As I get out of my car, he holds out his pamphlet once again. But I respond, as I have done all weekend, 'Sorry, dude, I can't today.'

I slam my front door behind me and immediately feel terrible. I am a creative and was once unknown, too – only wanting someone to look at my work, not even necessarily buy it, just see it. I know what it means to put something out into the world in the hope it will be seen by somebody, anybody. As I shower and attempt to watch some trash movie to distract myself, I can't stop thinking about the kid downstairs. With a sigh, I get changed and head back out the front to the gallery next door.

There he is. As I reach for his pamphlet and make my way inside, it's impossible to stop the smile spreading across his face. Walking around the gallery looking at his artwork, I fire questions that he dutifully answers. His name is Jaiden, he's from Newcastle and is a dishy at a pub. He taught himself to paint by borrowing books from his local library and when he finally grew confident in his style, decided to put on a show. Certain that Melbourne was the hub of creative forces and that holding a show here would be the first step toward being a 'real artist', he saved for months to pay for the flights, accommodation and gallery rental in order to, 'just get my artwork out there.' I love his style, but what I'm so impressed with is that he's hidden a turtle in every painting. He figured that if people walked past the gallery and saw those inside (like me!) engrossed in the artwork (searching for turtles), it would encourage others to come and see what all the fuss is about. G-E-N-I-U-S.

Not ready to buy a painting, but keen to help him promote his business, I ask for his Instagram handle.

'I only have this – no apps,' he says, showing me an old-school Nokia. Surprised, I ask how he booked his flights.

'I used a local travel agent,' he says. 'I like funding the community by supporting local businesses.'

By this point I am literally crying on the inside. Oh Jaiden, what a soul.

Once I'm back at home cooking up Sunday pasta (what else?!), I can't stop thinking about this amazing young guy. How hard he's worked, how vulnerable he's been, how determined he is to show up even if no one buys anything, and how he is staying at the crummy backpackers across the road that no one should ever really experience in their lifetime. What's $400 to me, I think, recalling his cute painting on the back wall of the gallery. I mean, yes, I have a small business and I really *could* use that money for something practical, but in my heart, I know the best way to spend it is on giving someone a moment of creative assurance.

Years later, that beautiful painting still hangs on my wall, a constant reminder to me of passion – and persistence. Jaiden's perseverance, even when the world said, 'No thanks, mate, don't have time,' is the essence of what it means to be a creative soul, to do everything and anything for the sake of passion and fulfilment, regardless of whether others say it's valuable or not. If you start to see hidden turtles in my work from now on, Jaiden, that's for you, pal!

THE PASSION COMPASS

Considering that our jobs play such a big role in our days, figuring out what interests us and fills us up is super important. I have spent a vast portion of my life on this planet learning what that is for me – I mean, who wants to go home and spend their only remaining leisure hours, between 6 and 10 pm, lethargic and unenthusiastic from a job that's slowly killing them? Certainly not I, said the fly.

Especially since learning I have ADHD, I've realised I have to work where my interests lie. It's critical. If something is not of interest to me then I'm not motivated to do it in the slightest. At the start, my first career – teaching – was interesting, but eventually the monotony and school politics drove me mad. When I compared my own efforts with how much over-and-above the other early-career teachers were giving, it was clear my level of interest didn't match.

Then, there was the question of creativity. For me, this is a huge deciding factor in my happiness. My innate nature is full-blown creative at 100,000 per cent capacity. I want to make things and paint things and use colour and create things no one else has done, to give others the gift of something exceptional and spectacular. I like spontaneity, no structure and the freedom and flexibility to be agile with my energy and move around wherever I want, for however long, working only with those whose energy is right for me. That is not the environment the education system functions in . . . *at all.* Actually, quite the opposite. No wonder I felt like I was walking around buzzing at half vibes – only 40 per cent of me was in the room.

All jobs will deplete you to some degree, no doubt, but if you feel as though this is constant, then maybe consider how much of 'interested you' turns up to the job or project. If you work full time between the ages of 18 to 65 you will dedicate 94,000 hours to your job. Do you want to spend nearly 100,000 hours of your life feeling drained, uninspired, not yourself or in unrest? Some of us will spend more time working than any other aspect of daily life, so why make it unenjoyable activity that drains you of your two precious life forces: time and energy?

When I asked myself these questions I got a resounding, 'NO THANK YOU, MA'AM. Lemme try something else.' So, I left a fulltime teaching job in search of a soul-filler – for Plant Mama.

These days, I feel certain that no money or job title is worth the emotional and physical drain of feeling below the point of terrible just to make a few bucks. Just like a long list of people I know, I'm no stranger to having sabotaged my life and body just to maintain a job I accepted years ago, but no longer have any interest in. We behave as if keeping society's expectations of maintaining the same obsessions and career path is easier than honouring our true selves, which undeniably takes more courage and guts. You can change your passions, career, interests, pleasures, people, etc. at any time you'd like. In fact, I'd be rather bored if I laser-focused on just one thing. When we rest all our fulfilment on only one job, activity or person, we sabotage our future happiness, because we've thrown all our eggs into one basket that is inevitably going to tip over at some point, leaving us lost. We must gather a variety of 'joy-fillers' from multiple tanks.

FROM THE CABBAGE PATCH

Before we get into how I turned my passion into a business and lifestyle, let us wind back the clock to where it all began . . .

Li'l Miss P Mami shot into this world circa January 1990, joining Ma and Pa Holmes and brother Cameron on a quarter-acre of Queensland paradise. With quiet streets, friendly neighbourhood kids, a backyard veggie patch, huge home garden and lots of outdoor space, it was everything a hyperactive, creative kid could ask for.

Though lovingly married, my parents could not have come from more different backgrounds. Born on the family farm, my Aussie-born dad grew up in a hard-working, respected local family. He had lots of freedom, finished school, got a trade, travelled the world, acquired a degree, found a wife, settled down and had a family. He may have experienced some bumps on the road, but in general, he's had a pretty cushy ride.

On the other hand, my mum emigrated from Iran in 1970, age 12, to a pineapple farm in Queensland. None of her family had ever seen a pineapple or worked on a farm. Apparently, Ahmed, my grandfather, turned up to his first day of work on the farm dressed in a full suit and shiny black shoes. He soon learned, and every time I pick the perfect pineapple from the bunch, I quietly thank him for this skill.

Pre-teen Mama Holmes spoke no English, was bullied relentlessly every day at school and kept under an intense home regime by strict Iranian parents. At 16, she ran away. She moved cities, became homeless, jumped from streets to friends' couches, took low-paying jobs and found herself at the end of *many* terrifying and stressful situations. But, through perseverance, grit and resilience, she eventually made her way forward in the world, found my dad, fell in love . . . and here I am.

Being exposed to these two vastly different life paths has taught me about the personal responsibility of using your early experiences to shape your life's direction and future. While both of my parents started out in extremely different circumstances, they each ended up creating a joyful life through awareness, personal choice and hard work.

As I entered high school, my mum started a business as an event organiser with a side-hustle as a life coach, learning initially from the best: Anthony Robbins.

Don't roll your eyes! He's intense, but brilliant. Through her learnings, words and actions, Mum taught me from a very young age that we are all 'captains of our own ship'. She would say that if I was unhappy with where my ship of life was heading, then all I had to do was steer the rudder toward a new place. And if that didn't feel right either, then I could keep changing course again and again. Eventually, she said, I'd gain an understanding of which path allowed me to sail the happiest, easiest and most freely.

I have sent my employment and passion ships across many rough seas and found myself gripping onto that helm for dear fucking life. There is nothing more soul destroying than feeling lost and stuck in the middle of a career ocean that *you* chose to sail into; the university degree that took *years* of your life and huge expenses of your time and money, only to find that when you started working in your 'dream career' you were alienated and destroyed by the thing you so desired in the first place. Worse still, when the penny drops that the pay rate you spent years building will disappear when you start at the financial bottom in a new and exciting industry – you want to vomit. I know it and I understand it. It's a huuuuuggge risk. But, what is better: a richer you or a fuller you? I know rich people and they are not any happier, so I choose fuller.

When I enrolled at university in Brisbane to become a high school teacher, I genuinely believed I would be in the classroom for the next 40 years. I had no inkling that this career choice would single-handedly drain me of my life force and that within 10 years of graduating I would have left it far behind and instead be running a creative company, working with amazing people and getting paid to gallivant across Australia. Some of us assume that our chosen course or career path has one direct line forward, or that we only have one 'big passion' in life that we must identify and pursue. However, we forget that over time our environment, needs, desires and interests can change or fade – and drain our energy as they do.

> **What is better – a richer you, or a fuller you? I know rich people and they are not any happier, so I choose fuller.**

From my late teens to now, I have flicked that rudder to change course over and over again, filled with tears and fears every time. And yet always, soon after, I locate a more grounded, stronger and better-informed human on the other side. I am currently the main character of a life that I never knew existed for me, solely based on assessing where I am at a particular moment, deciding on where I want to go and changing course to get there.

PASSION KILLER

I took the classic route from high school to choosing my university degree based on two things: 1) I would rather cut off my left tit than go work in an office building, and 2) I loved playing sports. The things I loved doing as a child – classic career-coach move to say look at these to figure out your career path – didn't offer any clarity. If being Sister Mary Clarence from *Sister Act 1* was an option, I'd have chosen that! I spent my entire childhood creating things: sewing wrist cuffs, taking photos, gluing sequins to belts, making mix CDs with a stunning LimeWire library of ripped tunes, and creating an array of after-school snack options. These didn't seem like great job prospects when it came time to pick a uni degree, so instead I chose something physical . . . (fast forward to now, though, and it turns out the career counsellor might have been right).

Back in high school, my parents paid a specialist career person to assess my personality, interests and grades. He very pointedly advised *against* me being a teacher, saying I would get bored in a few years and I would work best in something creative, managing myself. HA! As always, the Universe sends us messages: whispers at first, then louder and louder, until we're forced to listen.

In the last months of my final year before graduating from uni, all of us trainee teachers were required to do a stint of supervised teaching in classrooms, applying our learnings in vocational placement. Once completed, this 'final prac' would give us sign-off on our teaching ability. I was placed in an enormous elite all-boys school whose students had a certain reputation, so I had some idea of what I was heading into. Whenever the boys handed me notes in class with their numbers to 'call them' or made jokes to their mates about my tits, I ignored them; I knew my place as an early-career teacher. 'I can grin and bear it for long enough to finish my prac and get out of here,' I told myself.

The Universe sends us messages: whispers at first, then louder and louder, until we're forced to listen.

Nearing the end of my placement, it was finally Friday lunchtime. The bell had gone for students to move to last period and I was cleaning up skipping ropes from the gym floor after the Year 8 class. As I bent down, I noticed a bunch of boys laughing and then my supervising teacher screaming at them rather intensely as he gestured at them to move off. He was still furious as I approached, so I asked him what had happened. He had caught the boys zooming in on their phones to film a close-up of my arse as I bent down. He was incredibly angry and assured me the problem would be dealt with.

In shock, I walked to collect my things for our next lesson, tears silently falling down my cheeks. When I returned to my desk, I was told to go to the deputy principal's office. I was relieved, assuming that as a female in her 60s she would offer a supportive and empathetic place to share my distress. WRONG. The next four minutes would go on to destroy how I felt about myself at work for the next decade.

As soon as I sat down, she told me I would need to leave the school immediately; she considered it an inappropriate lapse of judgement for me to have been given a teaching placement at an all-boys school due to 'how I looked' and my age. I asked what had happened with the video. She said it had been deleted and the boy sent back to class. Meanwhile, I was to be transferred to another school to begin my prac all over again. I was asked to leave her office, pack my desk up and immediately exit the campus.

Never in my life have I experienced more shame than in that moment, and from then on, I carried a belief that schools don't support their teachers. This unfortunately became my experience in the years that followed, tormented by school politics that prioritised parent 'clients' over staff support. I look back now and see myself quietening down who I was (and am), as if to avoid causing ripples. In my early years of teaching, I often found myself in schools where things played against my morals, but felt unable to say anything, haunted by the notion, 'many people would kill for your job'. On reflection, it's clear I was never meant to be a teacher because I never thrived in that environment. I was made to feel smaller and didn't respect many of the decisions my bosses were making, so it was never going be a functioning work environment for me.

Even before I came to these realisations, however, I had started to feel irritated, disinterested in teaching the same old 'Intro to AFL' lesson. As I began to itch, I looked around and noticed two distinct personas among the teaching staff.

Let's call the first one Brenda. Brenda was *born* to teach. She *loves* kids and *loves* education and has patience, passion and brings wonderful vibes to all classrooms. We all love Brenda and we learn the most from her. In her early career she was a phenomenal teacher and remains so today. Actually, she's better, as she's retained her enthusiasm and grown her wisdom.

The second is Susan. Susan signed up for teaching because it seemed like a sensible and safe degree. She wasn't passionate about anything, but liked maths, so teaching seemed a simple solution; maybe her parents were teachers. At first, teaching was semi-enjoyable, but once the shine wore off (after the third year when she realised her pay wasn't going to increase much beyond where it was now and the kids were starting to get on her nerves), she actively started disliking the entire teaching experience. She considered a new career, but didn't want to forego the holidays, regular pay, super and long service leave she'd built up, only to start again at the bottom. So, she schleps through each school week bringing her shitty energy with her.

I'd bet we've all experienced both these kinds of teachers and experienced how their passion, or lack thereof, affects our ability to learn. Eventually, after a few weeks of reflection and assessing my nine-year teaching journey, I saw very clearly that unless I made some swift changes, Susan's destiny would soon be mine and I'd be doing a disservice to the job. I knew the power of having passionate, enthusiastic, positive-energy Brendas in the classroom and felt that my teaching role needed to be filled by one of them. If I had a child at this school, I thought, I would want them to have all Brendas.

Teaching is a two-way energy street. Teachers both give and receive from students; each work for the other. When I couldn't show up to my teaching role with passion, I knew – for my students and me – it was time to move on.

THE SPARK

I'd finally left my job in Brisbane and was looking for a shake-up. My then-boyfriend and I decided to move cities and as he had already lived in Sydney and my brother was in Melbourne, the latter became the obvious choice. After a while, I started noticing creatives out at play. They worked differently, moved differently – each with a side project or creative hustle complementing their main gig.

As I saw people functioning within their lanes of genius in a flexible, agile work environment, I began to absorb the possibility of this life existing for me, too. It fortified me with hope as my teaching career was crumbling, while at the same time supported my confidence with the idea, 'if I fail, I can just come back'. I think that's a genius concept for us all to hold onto. Through many changes, it has given me the faith to drive forward. Most doors never really close behind you. YOU CAN JUST COME BACK. So, you left your HR job to start a candle business and it did not work out . . . well, just go back to HR. It's better to have tried than to have not.

Of course, I would be an inconsiderate nuffy to not consider the scary depths some people might face when leaving a great job in a scarce industry where 'just go back' may not be an option. The way I see it is, something beyond your wildest understanding could be available to you at the other side of that risk. Are you going to take a peek to find out, or is that risk too great? It's a tough choice because there are no guarantees of something magical on the other side – remember, I am a realist too.

The way to approach it is to consider where you are right now against where you want to be and identify whether the scary leap to new potential is a *better option* than where you are right now. To me, it's that simple. If your new venture doesn't work out, at least you won't spend the next thirty years *wishing* you had become a Las Vegas showgirl – 'cause you darn gone tried it and it wasn't the cake or the cream.

The decision to leave my secure and stable job was not one made easily or without considering the risks. However, the choice to languish in teaching was far scarier and life-jarring than an attempt in any other direction. I knew deep down, if I continued to live a life that neither challenged nor inspired me, imminent death of my soul and energy would occur. I left teaching knowing that if, after a considerable amount of time, my search landed on nothing, then I'd just pull out my lunch box and whiteboard markers and return to exactly where I'd been before. Back to square one. Which is fine! I'd rather be on the court playing the game than in the seats watching it unfold. Eight million times over.

If you sit in shit for too long, it stops smelling. So, act before this happens to you.

FIVE SIGNS YOU'RE IN THE WRONG CAREER:

- After 10 hours of sleep, you wake up tired.
- You live purely for the weekends because weekdays are unfulfilling.
- While at work, you are constantly daydreaming of other things.
- You're only sticking it out for the pay cheque.
- Work training/development? Bury me now with live cockroaches.

plant
mama
www.plantmama.com.au
PLANT DESIGNER
STUDIO FOR HIRE

NAVIGATING THE CHANGE

Your path doesn't need to be fancy or grand in intention, but rather, should follow what sparks your interest. Little curiosity gems are embedded in you and sparkle in reply to your soul's purpose – let them be your guide.

P Mami is an extension of my personality, strengths, experiences and purpose, developed over time. Through my varied jobs in the gym, retail, education, nannying, Ubering, landscaping, small business and art worlds, I grew to understand my work self and its impact on my satisfaction and fulfilment. With each change in uniform came a better sense of 'me at work'. Over time, I learned to productively identify which factors to remove and which ones to combine to generate my work genius and fill my satisfaction radar. As I pulled those things together with what I loved about the world, it set me buzzing.

We all need to make a living somehow, so considering how work impacts your life outside of it and vice versa can help you discover what's missing and what additional things can help elevate how you feel while at work. You don't need to aggressively quit your job or throw yourself into hosting private pasta dining experiences to locate your personal P Mami within, just consider this:

- Does the majority of the work you do fill or drain you?
- Does it make use of your gifts and strengths?
- Are you ready to consider answering the niggle for more in life – a deeper and richer experience that fosters your most elevated self as you operate in your specific lane of genius?

I have found that simply writing out the answers to some of these bigger questions helps me see my experience from a bird's eye view. Not in my head, gut or heart, but on paper and in front of me. You'd be surprised by what appears on the page as you release the thoughts and feelings buried deep within.

WHEN ASSESSING A CHANGE IN CAREER PATH, CONSIDER THE FOLLOWING:

- How do you feel before you go to work and then when you leave it – excited or hesitant?
- The way you talk about your job to others – is it positive or negative?
- Do you respect the person or the company you work for?
- How much of your energy is enthusiastically given to this role?
- How does this job or passion impede your health, relationships and social life?
- Do your work hours match your optimal hours of energy output, i.e. are you a night worker, flexi-creature, etc?
- Which tasks are easier or harder to complete? Of the harder, are you gaining skills and accomplishing these challenges eventually, so they feel worthwhile?
- What strengths and weaknesses did you bring with you to this job?
- Do your employer and colleagues support your gifts and talents?
- If the pay rate dropped tomorrow, would you still turn up?
- If your work team dropped out tomorrow, would you still turn up?
- How does your work contribute to your personal growth?
- Is your effort level generally meeting your fulfilment level?
- If you lost this position tomorrow, what would you do instead?

Don't underestimate the power of feedback from those you trust.

Answering these questions will allow you the space to consider not only how you work but, more importantly, how you *feel* when you work and whether there is any passion there.

Finally, don't underestimate the power of feedback. While it isn't always pretty, feedback is *the most important* element of them all. The people who know you well and work with you can be valuable mirrors, reflecting your strengths, weaknesses, habits and ways of working – all of which is super useful data that can deepen your understanding of where your natural interests lie.

WHAT IS PASSION, ANYWAY?

Passion is far beyond work and can show up at any moment of the day. It appears in our spare time and surfaces during excited conversations. Among these moments, you will find a consistent and common thread: the itch that needs scratching. Let's use my good friend Lila as an example.

We're in Carlton on a Thursday night at 9:10 pm, which is way past my bedtime – but hey, Lila has hit me up and I want to be there for her as she's in need of a chat. Funny and enthusiastic, Lila has a boring office job in marketing for a well-known Australian brand. She enjoys her job most of the time but, unable to put her finger on her unrest, she blames certain parts of it on her workload. Oddly enough, when we dissect it, these elements are not actually that bad or stressful, so we keep digging. Finally, we realise that Lila's unrest is due to her creativity being completely exhausted by her work, leaving her nothing for herself. All her creative ideas and juices are being injected into her job, which she loves but is starting to resent as it drains her of her most precious resource. Unable to fill her creative and passion tank effectively leaves her feeling deflated.

At this point, it's time for me to jump in. As her good mate and first-hand participant in her most enthused conversation topics, I know that Lila loves ceramics. Ever since I've known her, she's been whingeing about wanting to reclaim this hobby. So, with her current job unrest and my insider knowledge on hand, I suggest something that could help: enrol in a pottery class once a week to ignite some passion and creativity outside of work. Using Google, we find one close to her house and the next week she begins her classes. OH BOY, did I see my fun friend come back after *just* the addition of a one-hour pottery class each Wednesday that fed her soul.

Lila actively went and found something that ignited her passion and creativity and it shifted her back into alignment. The pottery class rejuvenated her creativity and she no longer felt drained by work. Eventually, the unrest and search for a passion project subsided as she continued to draw joy and creativity from her weekly hobby. Lila did not need to quit her job and open a ceramics shop to regain passion in her life, she just needed to follow the thing that made her feel good, regardless of whether it paid her bills or not.

Not everyone needs to make money from doing what they love – it's perfectly okay to go and work your normal job and add enriching experiences to your life, on the side. Some of us have turned our passions into work, but that doesn't make us better – maybe a little crazy, if I'm honest. For some, the very act of making an income from something they love would destroy the joy in it. In my mid-20s, I sold all my cameras and shut down my photography business when what was initially a passionate obsession became an overwhelming business that soon became a hassle.

I have landed in this current soul-filling destination because I have tried one million things. Name it and I have done it, or a close version. I'm also aware that many people simply do not have the option to choose what they do for work. I recognise the privilege bestowed on me and do not take it lightly or without gratitude. Yet, I find it interesting to observe that most people I know, after several years of being in their dream high-powered job that they chased for so long, often seem to lack passion. Does it dry up or is it that we constantly need to redefine ourselves?

You are the driver of your life, not a passenger.

A dream job does not necessarily equal passion or even fulfilment, it might just be the task that you like best out of everything else you could be doing for eight hours a day. I just happen to be one of the people that fought hard to bring my passion into a business. I realised that passion is linked to my dopamine train which is linked to my energy and my focus. So, if I want to make money – I need to be passionate about what I am doing. Simple, simple.

But how do you KNOW if you are meant to stay in your job and find a hobby, or jump ship altogether? There are no crystal balls here, only shit sandwiches in every direction. It would have been hard on me if I had stayed in teaching just as it was hard on me starting my company, I just had to decide which shit sandwich I was okay with eating. Did I want to operate at half vibration forever or did I want to be stressed but in alignment? Have the security of working for someone else, or the freedom of running my own ship? I chose to ditch the concept of consistent income and security and replace it with following my passion and freedom, eventually culminating in P Mami Industries.

If these ideas are sparking thoughts in you, why not open that door and follow the niggle? It might end up being a passionless pursuit and a small waste of time and money, but what it serves you in return is useful information. Each redirection or failed hobby is a step closer to the right one as you eliminate the factors that do not light a match in you. My success has occurred purely because I opened every door with a passion niggle then closed those that didn't work for me. Eventually, I landed on the P Mami door and am now happily residing in my room (and passion) for the next few decades, or until I get bored again, which up to now, has happened every six years. So, watch out!

Gandhi, Oprah, Anthony Robbins and any other worldly philosopher will tell you the same thing: the journey of self is the only teacher, so quit asking us! The only person who has all the info on everything pertaining to you is YOU. So start getting friendlier with yourself and your passion. Get comfy and buckle up please, your future self will thank you (and me) for pushing you toward a more passionate and satisfied version of yourself. Remember always: you are the driver of your life, not a passenger.

SEEKING A SOUL-FILLER

It is entirely possible for you to do anything you want. You can open any business, work in any field, try any passion project or light a match and burn all expectations as you wait for your next calling. That said, I need to warn you that if you choose to join our cult of career burners and passion pursuers then know this: things will get hard and you will lose sometimes more than you win. But, you will never regret the trust fall, whatever lies at the bottom. Everything is a lesson.

If you take this path, many of your family and loved ones will think you are nuts, no doubt about it. I have incredibly supportive parents, but they were terribly concerned about me and my financial security and future as I worked like a nutso on Plant Mama. I had to face the idea of 'embarrassment' if everything went belly up. I knew *nothing* about running a business and I certainly didn't have a) my shit together or b) a plan of what I was going to do. All I knew was what I *didn't* want to do.

Wanting to save face is what holds a lot of people back and it's human to feel like this. We are born into a world that instinctively makes us care about what the tribe thinks of us. It's innate, but it does not need to be followed. If you can push past the initial fear of what others think (remembering that no one particularly cares what you're doing anyway), you can be free to test the waters.

My passion for plants was sown and grown by my parents as we had a huge backyard and veggie patch, and while I denied the need and requirement for nature ('cause it wasn't cool) in my teens and early 20s, soon the desire to fill my space with green made its way to the surface. Before I started a plant business, I was just a li'l ole gal collecting and cultivating a wide variety of plants in her home. I'd spend my weekends at plant sales, scouring online marketplaces for second-hand plant bambinos, buying books on plants and speed-dialling Mum for tips and advice on my growing plant famiglia. See how curiosity led to my passion?

You take a risk when you decide to leave what's regular and consistent in your life in search of nothing but unpredictability as you start something brand new. HOW FUN FOR ANXIETY, HUH?! Sometimes you'll encounter people who will be uncomfortable as you search for clarity, agitated by their own feelings. It niggles at them as they watch you. Some people are not yet ready to face their own unrest, so they reject it. And you. I like to use these people as fuel to my fire, a reminder that I am courageous as I chase down what's calling my soul.

Leaving something stable but draining in search of something new but fulfilling will gift you the opportunity to spend all 24 hours of your day as close to an aligned self as possible.

But, the positive counter to all this is: leaving something stable but draining in search of something new but fulfilling will gift you the opportunity to spend all 24 hours of your day as close to an aligned self as possible. Rather than denying its existence because it feels uncomfortable, I know that pursuing curious moments is the breeding ground for growth. To unleash the lesson, we must step forward freely, eager and ready to uncover what this shift in energy, curiosity and passion will unveil.

Ultimately, this is what we should be attempting as our daily goal: to use our gifts as we serve our soul's purpose while managing our energy intake and expenditure as we practise a life that delivers pleasures by the bucketful. It won't come without a few pails of pain, but nonetheless it'll be an enjoyable experience overall.

EXPLORE
THE
PASTA-
BILITIES

USE YOUR ENERGY WISELY

> Somewhere between burnout and I-can't-be-fucked is a sweet spot where, over time, your efforts and energies will repay you.

For all I've said in this chapter so far, passion ain't all of it, my friends. One of my favourite quotes of all time is: *hard work beats talent when talent doesn't work hard.* BA-BOOMBA. Don't get me wrong, hustle culture is not something to be glorified and I have blurred the line and overworked on countless projects, putting my health on the line to do so – do not recommend. What I can say, though, is that somewhere between burnout and I-can't-be-fucked is a sweet spot where, over time, your efforts and energies will repay you. Basically, if you want ultimate gains then you must put in ultimate pains – or the work, at least.

There was plenty I *didn't* know when I made my Melbourne move, but I *was* smart enough to realise that it would be impossible to birth my Plant Mama business and pay my bills at the same time. Unless you have rich parents or a giant wad of back-up cash, you must be willing and able to work another job that gives you sufficient space and time to build your business. Plant Mama did not pay me one dime for at least three years, so it was my other work and side hustles that floated my over-priced Richmond rentals and inflated Melbourne living expenses, like $24 avocado on toast and $7 chai lattes.

While Plant Mama built jungles on the weekends, she needed to work for more reliable cash during weekdays. For a good while I kept a hand in both sides of the game: casual relief teaching for two-to-three days and part-time nannying for the others; weeknights and weekends working as an Uber driver zigzagging people around Melbourne in my silver Suzuki Swift. I had the best playlists, the best chats and handed my Plant Mama business cards to any passenger that asked what else I did for work. Which was *everyone.* My Uber talents were unwavering and if you wanted to get from Collingwood to South Yarra in under 30 minutes, I WAS YOUR WOMAN. I knew all the backstreets and shortcuts, engaged in interesting conversation and offered mints and water, ensuring an enjoyable experience for all.

I was a busy, small-biz gal working eight days a week as I jumped between working on Plant Mama, nannying Mila and Aj after school, teaching one day and waitressing at a random 50th birthday the next, selling kombucha at the Saturday morning markets and Ubering in between it all. Ask my friends how many weekends they saw me for the first four years of building Plant Mama, or how many parties I attended, and the number would fail to fill one hand. My lack of dopamine in teaching had meant I'd favoured partying on the weekends; however, once my dopamine ignited with Plant Mama, I no longer desired the weekend-only-focused existence or the hangover!

I knew very early on in my business that momentum builds momentum, that if you want something to be more productive and effective as it moves forward, then you need to *keep going.* As things move faster and keep developing, they gain their own energy and are harder to stop. So, to achieve continuous growth, apply constant effort. I worked like an animal seven years ago and I worked like an animal seven seconds ago, so incredible business opportunities continue to appear in my favour within short periods of time. I have never wavered in my dedication and determination, always showing up, always giving my best, sometimes more.

Being unending and unstoppable allows the gates to keep opening in your favour. While we need to restructure the concept of the word 'hustle,' I believe in the depths of my soul that second to the strength of my creativity, the energy that powered my success was my sheer ability to work hard toward something I loved. The more I enter the world of hiring people, the more I have realised there are two types of people in the workforce. Those who go to work, and those who work. I am the latter and only employ those who are, too.

All of that effort created a powerful and energetic force, which was the push behind Plant Mama's success, culminating in one unstoppable machine. What's nice to notice is how Plant Mama ran so Pasta Mama could walk – the way that the mama of plants worked her little tooshie off in the beginning so that the angel of pasta could take on the shortcuts, slow down, absorb the past lessons and execute something more streamlined. My best work-self was there all along, I just had to try a few different combinations before she revealed herself to me.

When you follow a call with powerful action you may discover that passion is often the by-product of exploring your curiosities. It's not necessarily a BIG BANG catalyst that's instantly obvious and all-consuming, rather an experience that ignites a spark which slowly builds a deep love, leading you toward a more interesting life. There is nothing more comforting and energising than living in alignment; a life of passion-filled pursuits, whatever their size and form.

When you follow a call with powerful action you may discover that passion is often the by-product of exploring your curiosities.

IT'S ALL IN THE TIMING

Let me tell you a little story that changed the trajectory of my life forever – one that landed at the perfect time.

I had just finished one of my very first plant jobs at a hair salon in Toorak owned by a lady in her 50s. She was loud, friendly, robust, assertive, blonde, beautiful and tough, but in a really admirable and still soft way. I can't remember her name, which is classic of me – and a shame!

As I handed over my parting gift, a watering can, and made to leave she grabbed my wrist firmly and asked if I had a boyfriend. When I responded that we'd broken up about a year ago, she asked me my age.

'Twenty-six,' I replied.

'You know, Jen, I wish someone had told me this when I was your age because it would have helped me a lot. It's completely okay to focus on yourself and work hard on your business right now, while you have the energy and time to do it well. I am in my 50s now and don't have the patience or the focus to dedicate everything I have to this. I am old and have attachments, so what I have to give is minimal. Your friends will start having children soon and you might want to do that soon too, or maybe wait a bit, maybe not at all. But, this time you have is precious and wonderful and your energy should not be taken for granted. Your time to locate what you want is equally if not more important right now than creating a family, if decide you want to go all in for Plant Mama.'

WHAT A GIFT! With just a few well-timed words, this generous-hearted businesswoman set me up with the knowledge that with hard work at the right time, I can have both my dreams: a creative work pursuit and a family. It felt like a soul message, delivered right at the start of Plant Mama, and I ran with it.

When assessing the pros and cons of being P Mami, it's clear by a mile that the pros still outweigh the cons, for now. I expect the things I enjoy in my work now will not be the same in maybe three months or eight years. I have metamorphosed through many stages and cycles of industries, jobs and personas and through them all I have allowed myself to remain open to where the wind or Universe blows me. A mere three years ago I never would have expected to have something like Pasta Club in my possession and look at me now, working once again in an entirely different career field, born out of and guided by a teeny spark of interest and manifested through my energy and effort.

We are all able to generate our own Pasta Club momentum, formed by the heat of passion in motion. It is accessible to anyone active in their searching for what ignites an enjoyment light in them. When this all-consuming fire takes over, the risks feel small because the excitement feels so big.

PRINCIPLE 2
Passion

The Universe sends us messages: whispers at first, then louder and louder, until we're forced to listen. The more you resist something trying to be heard, the more it will persist.

Your most important daily decision is whether you want to be on the court participating in the game of life, or in the seats watching it unfold for everyone else.

Find what sparks a fire in you – the point where risks feel small because the excitement feels so big.

To achieve ultimate gains and consistent growth, apply constant effort to create momentum.

Ask yourself

What 5 things in your life provide the most excitement and enthusiasm?

What were you doing when you were 9 years old that was fun?

Do you need to be more active in hunting down what ignites the fire inside of you?

Do you prioritise time in your week for enjoying your passion – big or small?

Do you relate more to Brenda or Susan – spend your days feeling depleted or filled up?

chapter three

PLEASURE

THE HEART OF ALL THINGS

P-L-E-A-S-U-R-E is the life approach which guides everything I do. Oscar Wilde called simple pleasures the last refuge of the complex, and I could not agree more. As you begin to peel back the layers of P Mami you'll find pleasure at the centre of my mission – in business and in life. With every hard thing rolling around our world today, and also our minds, the safe space of lovely things helps keep us sane. The pleasure spectrum is endless and everyone's manifestation of pleasure is different, so respect each other. With pleasure at the heart of everything I touch, let me share how I seek out the simple things: in my fridge, by the sea and at the dinner table with friends. Welcome to P Mami Pleasuretown.

Obtaining pleasure and
delight from simple
experiences is the
fundamental ethos behind
every single thing
that I Mami creates.

SICILIAN SISTER ANGELS

I live by the Greek sage Epicurus' philosophy toward food and friendship, relishing the pleasure I find in them. Two amicas of mine – Eleonora and Freda from Sicily – are the truest representation of this approach I've met in this lifetime.

One day, while booking one of my recent trips, I come across Eleonora's farmstay on Airbnb, a biodynamic paradise that's been in the family for four generations. The first thing I notice, apart from the beautiful pictures, are the reviews. The descriptions of the wonderful host, her delicious food and the experience of her farm stir something in my soul, and although my trip isn't for a while yet, I make a booking. It's a very rare thing for me to lock things in so far in advance.

The moment I meet Eleonora and see her property, I'm instantly taken with how beautiful it is. Not in grandness, but in beauty, thought and nature – mostly because it has a fucking great energy and vibe. In her mid-40s, Eleonora works as a freelance designer and textile artist and sells Sicilian olive oil from the family farm. She shows me around the property then leaves me to get ready for dinner. I'm thrilled to find a copy of Anthony Bourdain's book *Kitchen Confidential* on the bookcase, something I've wanted to read forever, but alas, have never found time for. A Sicilian homestay seems like the perfect place to start.

As the sun is coming down, I take my book to the terrace and out of nowhere a tiny, furry, beyond-adorable dog comes ripping around the corner. Dearly missing my pup, Sprout, after six weeks away from home, I am pining for a canine companion and instantly fall in love with my new friend. Freda is her name – a stray dog and true-born hound angel that found her way into this home of love and is now a family member and shadow to Eleonora, much like Sprout is to me. Eleonora soon follows with a tray of appetisers, igniting a full-blown food convo as we fall down a rabbit hole of shared passions.

Eleonora explains that literally *everything* she cooks and makes comes from the land we are sitting on. The pasta we're eating is made from the wheat growing just metres away, the soap I used in the shower is made from the farm's olive trees, the eggs I'll eat at breakfast are from her chickens, the chocolate in our dessert cake is made from hand-ground cacao, and these black grapes I can't stop devouring have been plucked from the vine in the veggie patch. Anything not grown directly on the farm, Eleonora forages on her morning walks with Freda over the Sicilian hills: fresh tomatoes, walnuts, whatever ingredients she needs for that day.

I'm not surprised to discover that both Eleonora and her sister (who lives just down the road) contributed their story and recipes to *The Silver Spoon* (Italian bestseller *Il cucchiaio d'argento*). Eleonora embodies the full concept of eating what you grow while living off the land, with a canine mate right beside her . . . my dream life.

During my stay, as I watch her balance her corporate job with life's simple pleasures, I am so grateful to be experiencing this life first-hand – it blossoms into a genuine possibility for my own future. The connection between Eleonora, Freda and me makes this Sicilian trip extra special. I feel inspired, filled up and invigorated by my interest in this life and in cooking with the simple things.

As per usual, intuition nailed the brief on this one. This homestay has confirmed my soul's purpose, ten times over. It has reconfirmed my knowledge of the gifts available to us from the land – that through the act of savouring and appreciation, we become abundant in pleasures. *Ti amo* forever, Eleonora and Freda, my Sicilian sister angels.

A PLEASURE PHILOSOPHY

If we are not seeking pleasure amongst the fucked-ness of the world, then life would be one long and painful existence. I have cultivated a life with pleasure at the centre. My journey to find what stirs my soul and fills my heart is driven with the intention of only doing things that make me feel good 110 per cent of the time. Pleasure does not need to be grand and it doesn't need to be meaningful to anyone else but you. May I inspire you to claim your personal pleasures, whatever they may be.

By all means, share your pleasures with others – I certainly do! But, I urge you to follow the pleasure scent that calls to you specifically – not the one your husband likes or your best friend enjoys because keeping the peace is easier than saying, 'Hey actually, I don't really like camping and never have.' You can compromise, of course, and enjoy others' pleasures for the sake of seeing their joy, like getting your child a cat even though you *hate* cats. I believe, though, that apart from having pleasure experiences with other humans, which is a wonderful part of life, we must set out on our own adventure to discover what fills us up.

Pleasure does not need to be grand and it doesn't need to be meaningful to anyone else but you.

Life is about taking the twists and turns and, in between, finding good things that make the ride enjoyable. Have you ever had a cold beer after mowing the lawn? Or read a book under a palm tree at the beach? How about trying a freshly picked orange that's been cooled in the freezer so it's iced and fresh? Have you danced to ABBA in your living room with friends after a few lemon margaritas? Night nude swims in the Mediterranean Sea, solo? Oh, just me. Okay then . . .

Life has a funny way of handing us simple moments that fill up our energy tanks, but somewhere along the line we have stopped seeing them. Between taking care of ourselves and taking care of others we forget to do nice things for *us*. Joy, happiness and satisfaction will never be constant, but they *do* exist and you can obtain them by choice. Small joys are available to us during each day, otherwise the millions of people filling their gratitude journals would have been screwed years ago . . . and they are still going. Silver linings are always there and the more eager and able you are to see them, the broader your scope of gratitude, multiplying small joys to create big ones – like belly laughing with a friend after bawling your eyes out.

EPICUREAN DELIGHTS

What I've come to discover is that sometimes in life, people will arrive for a short amount of time and drop you little lessons or 'concept gems' that you need under your wing for the rest of the journey. This story is a beautiful example of how a short-lived connection can create an important long-term impact.

At age 23 I met a funny, bright and enthusiastic young lass who instantly made me laugh. She was what I call a 'five-second friend' – those people you meet and know, within five seconds, you'll make great friends with. The season of our friendship was golden but ultimately passed, as many youthful friendships do. However, two monumental 'concept gems' have travelled with me since that time, the first of which I'll share with you now.

My friend's dad, Chris, oozed intelligence and insight out of his eyeballs and toenails. His office was filled to the ceiling with books on every topic, a personal library that displayed all the information stored inside his brain, ready to be pulled out at any given moment. His interest in philosophy and self-improvement led our thought-provoking conversations whenever I joined the family around the dinner table.

One evening I was speaking quite passionately about my love for the Greeks and Italians and how attracted I was to how people lived in that part of the world. It was hard for me to describe at the time, but I felt deeply connected to the simple pleasures and ways of life intertwined throughout these cultures. Their friendly attitudes, unfussy foods, down-to-earth ways of living, beautiful surroundings and slower movement ignited an inexplicably strong interest in me.

Before I'd finished my enthusiastic monologue, Chris ran to his office, fished out the book *Travels with Epicurus* and gave it to me. At the time, I read through the first few pages but was distracted and left it unread for several years. Every time I moved house or travelled overseas, though, I always brought it with me. It was as if I understood that when I finally did read it, my world would shift.

When I eventually cracked open its pages and threw myself down the Epicurus hole, I discovered a philosophy that now underpins one of my most successful business ventures to date: Pasta Club. This book gave my idea breath. It allowed me to dive into history and fish out four compass points for life: 1) simple, 2) fulfilling, 3) connected and 4) whole. Whether Chris knew what he was starting when he gave me that book, who knows, but it undoubtedly began a warm fire within. The concept of obtaining pleasure and delight from simple experiences is the fundamental ethos that underpins *every single thing* that P Mami creates, and everything my team and I give to others.

As with many things, we have overcomplicated our idea of what pleasure is, creating distance between it and us. We deny ourselves lives full of pleasure because we've forgotten that what can truly fill us up are the simple things, accessible to all: a helpful friend, a soul-hitting song, a fresh cucumber with salt, a sunny day in winter. Epicurus taught me all this, so let me summarise the main points for you.

Greek philosopher Epicurus, born in 341 BCE, is famous for his approach toward happiness, friendship, tranquil living and pleasure. His central teachings – Epicurean Hedonism or Epicureanism – sought to maximise the *simple* pleasures in life, a concept that's been skewed over generations, replaced with the idea that hedonism is a form of overindulgent luxury. This was not Epicurus' mantra. He believed that a person should be able to eat a plate of salted boiled lentils and consider it the most exquisite thing in the entire world. He shunned cultures that added too much extra flavour to increase oomph, believing instead that the food's original and simple form, with just a dash of salt, is the most yummy and beautiful.

Epicurus valued old age as the pinnacle of life. To be in a position where you can safeguard your own happiness with a bucketload of wisdom in tow – *what a life!* I also adore the value he placed on friendships. He believed that friendship was human nature at its sweetest – that good friends will fill your pleasure-and-happiness tank tenfold. 'Of all the things that wisdom provides to help one live one's entire life in happiness,' he said, 'the greatest by far, is the possession of friendship.'

Epicurus bought a house in the country for all his mates to live in, something I fully intend to emulate when I reach my fifth decade. They spent their days reading books in the sun, laughing through intelligent conversations and eating bread, cheese and olives together while sipping wine made from the grapes on his land. Tell me: is this not the greatest philosophy and/or religion you have ever heard of? Pure pleasure!

Second to the pursuit of good mates, Epicurus valued the getting of wisdom. He believed that wisdom is pleasure in its highest form, far higher than bodily gratification, because wisdom is the key to understanding that simple life pursuits – friends, nature, seasonal food and the art of presence – are the *be all and end all*. Why, Epicurus would ask, are we all over there chasing the Gucci tracksuits

We have overcomplicated our idea of what pleasure is.

and gold-leafed caviar bumps when the best beach on the island is down that hill and Athena across the road makes the best moussaka in all of Kalamata?

Epicurus believed that the most desirable state in life is the one in which we achieve inner tranquillity and contentment from the simple things. I could go on and on about this man I love so dearly, but let's summarise a few key learning points from the pleasure and happiness king himself:

- **Be content with little and you will never want or need more.**
- **Gratitude will make you feel happy without effort.**
- **Both pleasure and pain are necessary to reach the sweet spot of happiness.**
- **Who you sit with at the dinner table is more important than what you eat at the dinner table.**
- **You only develop courage through adversity.**
- **Don't try and be popular – it's never what you want in the end.**
- **True pleasure lies in hanging with good people, not in materialistic items.**

How does this all connect to Pasta Club and pleasure? What did I drag out of Epicurus and his life philosophy and apply to my now-beloved dining experience? E-V-E-R-Y-T-H-I-N-G.

All the things that Epicurus identifies as pleasure-hitters are found woven throughout Pasta Club. Before it was born, I was having my close friends over for simple meals and meaningful conversations as we drank wine and listened to music: the sweet pleasures of life. These gem moments were so delightful, I felt we could not be alone in wanting to enjoy the wonderment of these joy-fests. So . . . I used my Plant Mama audience to guinea-pig an idea – would others want the same? THEY DID. So much so, that these nights, now known as Pasta Club, sold out over and over again.

What makes these fun-filled pleasure experiences so popular? Pasta Club is a loud, decision-free, simple-food focused, wine-pouring merry time, accompanied by loud disco music and a jungle of plants. All we ask of our guests is to focus their joy on who sits at their table and let us do the rest. Friends + simple food + fun conversations + light-hearted mood + freedom to enjoy with no time constraints + nature = Pasta Club (and pleasure!). I think Epicurus would agree, life doesn't get much better.

Blue Zones inspiration

If you were to ask Jenna/P Mami/Pasta Mama where her most 'pleasure filled' self comes out to play, the three would sing in unison: Sardinia and Ikaria. These two islands, one in Italy and the other in Greece, belong among the global phenomenon Blue Zones. They are also the two places in the world that simultaneously pull on my curiosity and pleasure strings.

Whether I discovered the islands first then learned about Blue Zones, or the other way around, is neither here nor there. What's more important is that they gave me the blueprint to develop P Mami and every glorious thing she practises. Like all my creative ventures, P Mami naturally evolved, so it wasn't until I was putting my thoughts down on paper that I realised my creative identity also revolves around nine core principles – the chapters of this book. As with all juicy P Mami goodness, ideas marinate over time, and then, magic!

At age 18, I first discovered Blue Zones while watching Oprah (duh!). Over the 45-minute episode I became completely captivated by her guest, Dan Buettner's theory. In 2004, as a *National Geographic* explorer, he was inspired to discover that Sardinia was home to a concentrated population of males over 100 years old. Intrigued, Buettner dug further and found several more populations – five in total – around the world with healthy centenarian populations, namely: 1. Ikaria, Greece; 2. Sardinia, Italy; 3. Okinawa, Japan; 4. Nicoya, Costa Rica; and 5. Loma Linda, USA.

Buettner called them: 'The Islands Where People Don't Die'. His study found that all five groups follow **Nine Power Principles**.

DOWNSHIFT

Downshifting is all about removing chronic inflammation through the activity of incorporating personal routines that reduce stress. This could be going for a walk with a friend, taking a break from work, some stretches, kitchen dancing, etc. It's about stepping away from what you are doing in order to recharge and reset.

MOVE NATURALLY

You won't find 97-year-old Nico getting sweaty at the local F45 class – no, no, no. He'll be walking the three kilometres down the driveway every day to collect the mail or purposefully taking the stairs instead of the ramp, and he'll spend *hours* working up a sweat in the garden, too. Blue Zones people exercise at low-to-moderate rates, but are consistent in their approach.

PURPOSE

The Okinawans call purpose *ikigai* which translates to 'why I wake up in the morning'. Dan and his team discovered that those who wake each morning with a set of goals or a purpose to motivate them are more likely to live longer.

EIGHTY PER CENT RULE

This concept is about finishing your food when you feel 80 per cent full as the brain can take time to register satiety. The 20 per cent is the deciding factor as to whether you maintain or gain weight.

PLANT SLANT

People in Blue Zones eat a mostly plant-based diet that consists of beans, nuts, green plants, fruits and vegetables. Meat is consumed but on rare occasions and in small amounts. Due to their isolation, most Blue Zones populations rely heavily on building diets around the idea of 'eat what you grow'.

WINE @ 5

Except for the Adventists in Loma Linda, people in Blue Zones drink wine regularly, but in moderation. One or two glasses of local wine are a daily practice – the trick is to drink it with friends or food, ideally both!

BELONG

The Blue Zones centenarians demonstrate a clear association between wellbeing and being part of a faith-based community, irrespective of the denomination. Belonging to a group that champions your ethos and offers support is important.

LOVED ONES FIRST

People in Blue Zones prioritise family. It's quite common to find elderly grandparents living with their children, as the family cohort supports each member by offering their love, presence and protection on a platter.

RIGHT TRIBE

What would life be without FRIENDS?! Blue Zoners choose social circles that nurture healthy behaviours and connections, recognising that one becomes most like those they are surrounded by. Okinawans formalise this practice from a young age, creating friendship groups called *moai* that commit to supporting one another throughout their lifetimes.

NOW, TELL ME HOW THIS IS NOT JUST WONDERFUL! If there were a religion for me, this would be it. These principles have not only proven to extend one's life, but also, help create a life of meaning, connection, purpose and pleasure infinite in delivery and consistency. We don't need to be on an island to feel or see this, my friends, it's as accessible to you in Toorak today as it was to Nico in Sardinia back in 1922.

As I have made my way through this list over my lifetime, some that hadn't initially seemed so important to me are becoming so now. 'Downshifting', for example, didn't exist in my world until my health forced me to do so, and my 'right tribe' adjusted over the years until I found 'the one'. Across the years, these principles have floated in the back of my subconscious, coming forth at times as a gentle reminder or sometimes a not-so-gentle one. Some are harder to implement than others, like always putting 'loved ones first' or following the '80 per cent full' rule when the extra 20 per cent is passionfruit gelato.

From the start, Blue Zones hit something special inside of me. Out of the many philosophies to smoosh my brain, obviously the right ones for me stick. In some strange way, as I watched Dan speak on *Oprah*, I felt like I was being told and shown something I was subconsciously and intrinsically connected to, but which in my current life I had yet to hear about. It was as if my soul was screaming, 'YES, YES. I BELIEVE THIS! I HAVE DONE THIS! THIS IS HOW TO LIVE,' but my brain was going, 'What are you talking about, sis? You ain't never been to Greece and Italy – calm down, yo!'

A few years later, I finally got my chance. In 2011, after winning $25,000 in a photography competition, I *finally* had the money to book a trip. Arriving in these countries for the first time was a true spiritual homecoming. The food blew my world, the people were warm and friendly, the houses and interiors idyllic, they had the best sharkless beaches I had ever seen and I loved the 'beach-bod positivity'. Ever since, that feeling of instant comfort and familiarity has dictated ALL my European trips. I have been to Europe five times and never once visited England or any other iconic country. Greece and Italy are *it* for me. So much so, that if you said I was constrained to only visiting those places for the rest of my life, I would be thrilled. If there is anything I can recommend for you to do once in your life, it's to take yourself to a Blue Zones location – especially to my all-time favourite place, Sardinia. (In the Places chapter I give you lots of juicy tips – take note!)

As I have moved through these countries, I have been overwhelmed by their expression of what it means to 'live life'. To slow down, to eat fresh food that's seasonal, to laugh with friends over wine every day at 5 pm, to spend time with your family and to take long, silent walks in the morning. Little did I know that my obsession at age 18 with Blue Zones would be the foundation of one of my biggest businesses: Pasta Club. All its wonder, research and understanding stayed silent under the surface until it made its way onto the tables of thousands of attendees eating my signature spaghetti sauce.

At the heart of my businesses and at the centre of our intention, has always been the recognition of the simple pleasures in life. Seeing a plant family grow slowly over time with Plant Mama, sharing a summer pasta with friends outside in the sun with Pasta Mama, connecting with a fellow business warrior over a similar problem in Sheilas Club. I am lucky enough to have intertwined my passion for pleasure and my business life, but your own simple pleasures are both abundant and yours for the taking. Be brave, follow their call.

THE FOOD–PLEASURE EQUATION

It's a Sunday morning and I decide to make some breakfast, which is rare as I am partial to skipping breakfast in favour of intermittent fasting, taking my first morsel around 10–11 am. Last night's dinner was as simple and as lazy as breakfast is about to be, but neither lacked flavour or pleasure. For dinner I ate the tastiest, creamiest and most perfectly balanced hard goat's cheese from Italy with chunks of freshly baked sourdough from Rustica, complemented with a few cold strawberries from the market, hot peppermint tea and an iced sparkling water with lemon from the backyard. It was 10:20 pm and I had just returned home after feeding 60 people, so I ate my feast lying in a steaming hot bath, watching *The Real Housewives of New York City* (nothing more comforting than trash reality TV, am I right?).

Breakfast will be similar: simple bits and bobs with a side of fruit – I love a palate cleanse at the end of every meal. This morning I'll make scrambled eggs with homegrown garlic, fresh eggs and expensive butter. The expensive butter is both necessary and absolutely worth its value when you are using such a small amount. Where possible, always, always, allllwwaays get the earliest-laid eggs into your trap, fresh is best. Until you have had a fresh egg fried in a dash of butter and with a sprinkling of salt, I am afraid you have not lived at all.

A quick analysis of my eating patterns and cooking habits reveals that there is an equation at play. Lazy + local + quality + simple = *la dolce vita*. *Lazy* meaning it must take less than 30 minutes to prepare, follow straightforward steps and use basic ingredients (nothing fancy here). *Local* meaning that, where possible, food should be accessed from my current vicinity as this means it will be both seasonal and community driven. *Quality* favoured above showmanship – I'd rather 200 grams of quality cheese over a kilo of factory cheddar, even if the homemade smaller portion costs more. When food quality increases, throw-in filler ingredients decreases. *Simple* means I embrace using fewer ingredients, focusing more on marrying the *right* flavours, not *the most*.

Lazy + local
+ quality
+ simple
= la dolce vita.

One of the recipes in this book, P Mami's OG Pasta, was a dish I literally threw together in my mind combining the five yummiest things: onion, balsamic, thyme, burrata and pangrattato. It has become one of our most famous dishes and was created even before I cracked open the pantry door. Based on its combination of ingredients, I KNEW it was going to be a hit. It is consistently one of the most requested Pasta Mama dishes of all time.

There are no fancy cooking-school certificates in my possession and if you saw me slice an onion, you'd die wondering how I have successfully fed thousands my famous red sauce in sold out Pasta Clubs across the country. When I am referred to as a chef I quickly counteract with 'intuitive home cook', because that is what I am. While I lack the skills to successfully remove a hot tray from an oven without copping a burn, I do know about the importance of food and how it builds connections and cultures. Healthy feasting fuels our bodies and nourishes our hearts – without it, we'd all cease to exist.

My obsession and admiration for Italian and Greek cuisine comes down to how my soul lights up during its consumption and in conversation. Between Epicurus' teachings, Blue Zones, my family's food influence and my soul bellowing to me, I have identified a set of commonalities that underpin how I cook and how I eat, placing pleasure and nourishment at the centre. My daily practice centres around the simple pleasures of cooking, eating and feeding, and Pasta Club is an extension this. Of course, I still order lots of UberEATS and buy lollies from the USA Candy shop on a weekly basis – it's unhealthy to be too restrictive – but overall, I look to consume food that provides pleasure, fulfilment, nourishment, energy and creativity as *easily* as humanly possible.

All my Pasta Mama recipes (some 'saved' by thousands) have no exact measurements and are just three or four steps. I am impatient with recipes that demand complicated methods and 8 million exotic ingredients. If my meal's not ready in under 30 minutes, takes more than six steps and uses anything beyond pantry staples F.O.R.G.E.T A.B.O.U.T I.T. I'll take some cheese and bread thaannnk you! I am too tired, hangry and irritable by dinner time to julienne my carrots or wait three hours for a lamb shoulder to cook. I want fast, simple, healthy and tasty food and I don't want to exhaust too much brainpower making it. Is that too much to ask? I think not.

Sometimes I think people forget that a piece of local fish cooked in lemon, butter and salt, with a salad of gem lettuce, shallots, parmesan and dill, and some fresh bread and butter on the side, is potentially one of the most delicious meals to consume in a lifetime. A work of art, from nature. And . . . so easy to make! With few ingredients and barely impacting the wallet. We need to remember that simple eats can be good, and in fact, are much better if we just learn the basics.

Pleasure is one of life's fundamentals – we all deserve it and need to prioritise it. It's what brings a spark to an otherwise ordinary day: a swim before or after work, a moment with your face in the sun before a meeting, a cry-laugh with an old friend, or a stranger propping open the door as you carry through your overspilling box of produce. Clearly, for me, pleasure is food, being in nature and connecting with people. It's spending time with friends and leaving each other a little bit taller. Perhaps for you it's something totally different – though I still hope to inspire you to notice the pleasure that comes from consuming simple food delights: a juicy strawberry, fresh bread, homemade coffee and a hot plate of Nonna's spaghetti. Pleasure should reside in each of our days, whether big or small. It should be a commandment served as the price to be alive. Enjoy it all.

Pleasure should reside in each of our days, whether big or small. It should be a commandment served as the price to be alive.

My food goddesses

Reflecting on the origin of my love affair with eating and with food, it boils down to two main things: family and a soul call. The food featured at my family's table is something I do not take for granted, especially when I watch some of my friends attempt to boil water or throw a salad together. I have three key food influences in my family and, unsurprisingly, it's the women: my mother Frances, her mother Fatima, the Persian cuisine queen, and my dad's mother Audrey, a classic farmhouse cook. Frances, Fatima and Audrey – my food goddesses. The intense level of joy, satisfaction and love I receive from cooking for those whom I care about is directly linked to this magical trio. Food is how they show love for others and I pay that forward to my community. Quite simply, food is love and I share mine with creativity, colour and simple pleasures.

Audrey was your classic Australian home baker and BOY, WAS SHE GOOD. Her jam drop biscuits and pumpkin soup recipes won the Pittsworth Best-in-Show prize a million times. She'd make fresh bread, curried steak, the *best* roast potatoes, pikelets with jam and cream, and brown sugar biscuits. We'd bake together all weekend when I stayed, my chubby little fingers pressing the biscuits flat. Audrey May and Jenna May. A forever bond.

My grandma Fatima cooks Persian only. When I was young, we'd visit every month, arriving to fragrant aromas and lots of organised chaos in the kitchen. Fatima does not speak much English, but what she does say is, 'Sit down, darling! How are you? Plate! Sit, sit, sit. Eat, eat, eat,' while she effortlessly grabs a huge hot pot of saffron and butter rice with her bare hands from the stove and places it on the table. My favourite dish of hers, without a doubt, is lubia polo (green bean rice), a Persian meal of small beef meatballs, green beans, rice and a to-die-for mix of herbs, lemon and saffron, which we'd shovel into our mouths with pure satisfaction. (Dessert, on the other hand, was some awful rock cake. I only had to taste it once to know I would never try it again.)

Fatima and Audrey were fundamental to Pasta Mama's inception, no doubt. However, my mum, Frances, is the real hero of this food story. She combined their talents to find a perfect balance between each of their cuisines, adding her own flair to the mix. My adoration for backyard-veggie-patch food comes from her, as the base of our childhood dinners was the deliciousness growing within plucking distance. That very same veggie patch still provides the goods to this day. Now, as then, once Mum has the main part of dinner under control, she nips outside with scissors to chop lettuce, cucumber, herbs and tomatoes straight from the vines into the serving bowl. Once rinsed, we devour them with lemon juice, olive oil and seasoning. YUMMO. Have you ever eaten a cucumber straight after it has been picked? Their crunch and sweet-savoury refreshment leaves their supermarket cousins for dead. My childhood taste buds were cultivated on the freshest of fresh.

Like every other mum out there, mine had *a lot going on!* However, somehow in the brief moments available, she managed to keep our family incredibly well fed and healthy. She shows us love in many ways, but the most practical way is through her food and cooking. This is her love practice – nourishment as a caring act for her family. Even now in my early 30s, whenever I visit home Mum is still thrilled to cook for me, to send me on my way with snacks, to make me a coffee and a biscuit as I work on emails and make calls. Mama Holmes taught me the basics of cooking and the pleasure of harvesting your own produce, but most importantly, she taught me how to love and care through food. How to nourish, to share, to connect and to taste with your inner circle. Simple pleasures. *Bellissima.*

Intuitive cooking for pleasure

When I say that 50 per cent of Pasta Mama is a soul thing, I really mean it. My food skills in the kitchen and ability to craft recipes come from an inner voice. I've always just whipped things together and thrown flavours in a pan directed by my unconscious mind and intuitive body. It feels like a dance over the stove, prompted by quiet but firm whispers: 'Keep stirring', 'Add more balsamic', or 'JUST TASTE IT!'

When you start out, cooking intuitively will take time to master. There'll be plenty of 'Whoops, added too much pepper' or 'FUCK, BURNT THE ZUCCHINI!' moments. But, never fear – true learning comes from making mistakes. So, just have fun! The sooner you trust the 'glug' of oil over an exact tablespoon measure, the sooner your stress in the kitchen will subside. Your tongue gives you the opportunity to test and adapt the recipe along the way, so just relax, add more of . . . whatever it needs. Cheese always helps.

My early hospitality career was working the register at La Porchetta, Toowoomba, when I was seventeen and now look! I'm cooking food for the heavy hitters. Food is meant to be fun, free and creative – an act of self-care. So, pull back on judging yourself for not serving Michelin-star-worthy meals! As you experiment, you will sometimes put too much salt in the pesto, and even the best of us is destined to fail at cooking gnocchi at least once in a lifetime.

Every so often, though, you will execute a meal that will *blow your food mind*. Once you begin to understand how vinegar and sweetness work together, or how to gauge the amount of pasta water you need to add to your rigatoni, you'll begin adding notches to your home-chef belt that will elevate the food experience all round. In the end, though, whether it's epic or foul, cooking is simply meant to be a wonderful experience full of tests, trials, tastings and temperaments. Cook with love and pleasure as the intention and let go of the outcome.

cook with love and pleasure as the intention and let go of the outcome.

To learn basic cooking skills and to consciously consume will ultimately provide you the opportunity to eat with pleasure on a daily basis – and who is refusing multiple foodgasms a day, huh? As we spend the rest of our lives shoving tasty treats into our gobs, I hope we can all recognise and pay our respects to what drives nourishment and connection between us: food.

Food pleasure principles

I see the cycle of food and energy so clearly: from it growing in the ground, to being picked by a farmer, to then landing on my table and in my belly. All steps of this process are as important as one another. As I appreciate my personal journey on the food train, it's been nice to arrive at an understanding of how my body uses food best. Everyone comes from different cultural food expectations, socio-economic backgrounds and locations, so some of these may not apply to you or be helpful. Keeping that in mind, let me introduce you to my broad food principles.

SIMPLE IS BEST

Have you ever had a slice of heirloom tomato sprinkled with a little white vinegar and salt? Or munched on fresh crisp lettuce leaves dressed in dill, lemon, olive oil and parmesan cheese? Well, take my word for it, they are a taste revolution created by the most simple and cheap ingredients. No caviar (or its price tag) here. If you educate yourself on flavour basics, then your ability to combine fewer ingredients and create explosive flavours will strengthen. So, focus on cooking simple food combinations with high-quality seasonal ingredients that take no time to cook.

QUALITY NOT QUANTITY

When you cook 'simple' meals you'll use fewer ingredients, so focus on quality. A burnt butter sauce made from pure ingredients will make a world of difference, as will choosing a fresh, locally grown peach instead of the supermarket's shipped from who-knows-where. You could spend all your money on imported seafood for your linguine, but have you ever had pasta with 18-year-old parmesan, olive oil and fresh chilli, instead? Buy less and buy better.

VEGETABLES MAINLY

Like my Mediterranean Blue Zones mates, I favour a predominantly plant-based diet with occasional animal protein by way of locally caught fish, hormone-free chicken and organic red meat. Most of my meals centre around an array of vegetables dressed in spices, vinegars and oils, fortified with grains, seeds and nuts. I admit that preparing veggies in a way that makes them interesting and tasty is something you need to learn, but once you do, your world will open up. You just need some pantry basics and practice.

SUPPORT LOCAL

This will take some research, but once you have established your go-to vendors you will be set for life. Hunt down your local farmers market for produce as it's often more affordable and always in season, which equals better flavour. You'll most likely be paying the person who grew it themselves, too, a win-win for everyone. Get your dairy and basic grocery items from your local deli and, for protein, support your local butcher and fish market.

GROW WHAT YOU CAN

Don't start sweating, you don't need to move off the grid and build a greenhouse with multiple Italian tomato varieties. If you have a patio or even a small corner inside, a pot of herbs is a good start. Whatever you can grow that works for you, do it. That small herb garden will come in handy more than you realise as you begin your food-growing education. To master this task is one of life's most fulfilling activities, even if it's just a few chives chopped into your Saturday omelette. Fresh is best. Grow what you can in the space that you have.

STOCK THE BASICS

I have the skills to throw *anything* together at *any* time when literally *nothing* fancy is available. You should always have the following in your fridge and pantry, as doing so will mean you're always covered for *multiple* dishes: garlic, olive oil, balsamic, butter, tomatoes, fresh and dried herbs, parmesan, onions, ricotta, packet pasta, dried chillies, canned tomatoes, cannellini beans and stock cubes. With these basics and the recipes in this book, you can create magic on command.

SHARE AND CONNECT

Sharing a meal with someone will teach you a lot about them – it's a vehicle for conversation and an opportunity to connect and learn from each other. Food allows us to nourish one another – to share a fresh peach with someone on a sunny day or make chicken soup for a neighbour in times of need is an act of love. You will always learn something around a dinner table, whether from the food on your plate or the people you're sharing it with. Even as an introvert who likes my dog most, I find that sharing food experiences with good people is the fastest way to fill up my cup. Guaranteed.

Most of us are munching on something at least three times a day, whether in the form of a meal or my favourite: a light snack. Without too much overthinking or restriction, I think it is important for us to consider how eating is a pleasure act, or rather – should be. Epicurus and Pasta Mama taught me the art of simple eating and the pleasure available to us all, even that plate of salted, boiled lentils.

I know not all meals have the capacity to be pleasurable because of time and life and empty fridges. But keeping a stock of pantry basics and learning the art of savouring a fresh fig with a tear of gorgonzola cheese and some honey is a gratitude gift, a simple pleasure capable of existing at least once a day for us.

May we all eat with pleasure and with good friends. *Bella vita*.

PRINCIPLE 3
Pleasure

Through conscious gratitude we learn to see the abundance of simple daily pleasures all around.

You must actively be the sole architect in finding and building your personal sources of pleasure.

It is impossible to experience a life of pleasure without pain, so find the time to appreciate the sun when it decides to shine, knowing that sometime soon, it won't.

Ask yourself

When I say pleasure, what parts of your world instantly come to mind?

Are you consciously aware of the gratifying and fulfilling moments in your life?

What 3 simple pleasures are present in your days? (Hint: morning hugs, a warm fresh croissant slathered in butter, dog kisses.)

Which of the 'simple pleasure' activities mentioned in this book sparked something in you? What achievable steps can you take to enjoy them?

Do you prioritise filling up other people's pleasure tanks before your own? Why? (Hint: on airplanes you must put on your own oxygen mask before assisting others . . . just sayin'.)

chapter four

PERSONALITY

WE'RE BORN TO BE DISTINCTIVE

Personalities – we all own one and we all gotta deal with lots of different ones each moment we're alive. Our personalities allow us to bring something unique to the world because we're each born to be distinctive. Discovering, developing and expressing your personality helps everything make sense, while relationships with others helps keep things interesting. Knowing yourself will gift you the ability to constructively direct your energy toward personalities that make you feel good – people who challenge, support, elevate, humble and reinforce you, without being asked. While the most important connection is the one you have with yourself, a solid group of mates helps, too – the ones that fill your mornings with sore cheeks thanks to laughs from the night before.

'I'm not giving up my personality for anybody, okay?'

—Cher

KNOW THYSELF

Hi, I'm Jenna. By now I reckon I've done all the tests and personality analyses in the world, mostly before I discovered my ADHD. It's all been interesting and most of it's been useful. Some of it's spiritual, some of it's psychological, other aspects are purely for the body, baby – I didn't train to be a PE teacher for nothing! Here's what I know so far.

I am a Rebellious, Introverted Generator who is an Aquarius with an Ascendant in Sagittarius and Moon in Sagittarius and I emit mainly Vata energy. Oh, and my Life Path Number is 6. Originally, I had plans to explain all that, but since there's a lot of other stuff I want to get through here and a heap of information out there, I won't. Since we're all on our own unique journey, I know you'll find your own tools and guides to help you figure out your personality and how you work best with others. Regardless of which path you take, it's about mastering your PPS: Personality, Physicality and Soul.

Personality: the combination of characteristics and behaviours uniquely and distinctly you.

Physicality: the food you eat, the environment you're in, the stress in your body, the sleep you get, your mind and heart.

Soul: the inner journey to discover your purpose through self-awareness using intuition and energy as guideposts.

No matter what I am reading or exploring, I'm looking to affect and improve these three key aspects. I've explored many different pathways, but it's safe to say there are hundreds of thousands of approaches. To find what works for you, get out there, explore, stay open-minded and take each one with a grain of salt. Finding those you connect with can really open up a world of knowledge and possibilities when it comes to understanding your unique personality traits.

As well as understanding yourself, it's equally important to understand how your energy interacts and plays off those around you. You don't need to believe in the woo-woo world to know that! There is nothing you will see me fighting for more than the concept of how your personal energy affects every space and place you move into. Everyone's energy impacts others whether they are conscious of it or not. (Hint: the ones not aware are normally not the ones you want to be around.) We are constantly exchanging energy through our words, our body language, our eye contact, our intentions, our breath, our emails, our facial expressions and blah, blah, blah – it's *in* everything and it *is* everything. Ignoring it only detracts from using it to your advantage.

When you are authentic, you create a certain energy which people want to be around, because you are unique. I feel that talks so much to P Mami – there is an energy surrounding her. That surrounds me. The two words most often used to describe me are 'energetic' and 'authentic' and what I take that to mean is: I generate and cultivate authentic energy. Who could ask for more, honestly?

EXTROVERTED INTROVERT

I am uber, uber passionate about understanding the personality labels of 'introvert' and 'extrovert', as I have been called both in my lifetime and finally found solace when I recently understood what I *truly* am: an introvert. If you hear someone claim to be a friend of mine and call me an extrovert, then run. Clearly, they don't know the real me (or they don't understand what an introvert is).

Over time the definitions of introvert/extrovert have been confused, with many believing 'loud' people are extroverts and 'quiet' people are introverts. That needs reframing. A more current definition describes these labels as the way you *recharge your energy.* By those terms: an introvert recharges by turning inward, feeling most comfortable when in their own company, and processes things best when alone; whereas, an extrovert requires social interaction to fuel their energy, preferring to process things in social settings and discuss them outwardly. As with many things, these labels operate on a spectrum. People can shift their state over time in different settings and there are also those described as 'ambiverts', who comfortably adapt depending on mood and situation.

What I've come to learn about myself is that I am naturally an introvert with a loud voice. I say that because people have mistaken my loud voice and highly energetic personality as extroversion, but it's not – it's my personality (and ADHD). Recently I came across a phrase that perfectly describes me: the 'Extroverted Introvert'. Such people are introverts at heart and get drained by most people; however, in certain circumstances around *the right* people, they appear extroverted and energised.

HALLELUJAH, THIS IS MY TRUTH! I either feel completely drained by people or like Superwoman after seeing you, the latter being less probable. When I find myself behaving in an extroverted manner, I know I'm with the right folk, because they recharge me with their humanness . . . rare, rare, rare! In my early 20s I behaved like an extrovert and felt very disconnected from myself. I hung out with the wrong people with the wrong energy and, in the process, depleted myself completely. These days, people at Pasta Club see me as the life of the party, so I can still bring it, but now it's on my terms.

My introversion also explains how tiring teaching was to me, how *exhausted* I was *all of the time.* I would wake up tired after 10 hours of sleep and needed a nap every day after school for an hour, only to go to bed a few hours later at 9 pm. I was eating right, exercising and not really too stressed as life was pretty straightforward and mundane, but I constantly felt as if I were a zombie walking around, drained of all energy. My fellow female teachers who were 40-plus years old with families and children were bubbly, bright and on task, but me? I was 25, healthy, really fit and desperately in need of a 30-minute nap under my desk whenever I could steal the chance.

For me, being an introvert and spending eight hours meeting with 200 people a day – 180 students (six lessons of 30 kids each) plus around 20 or so teachers during my 'breaks' – was not a rejuvenating experience. YEAH, NO SHIT, SHERLOCK! No wonder I was so tired. At the time, I was completely unaware of how I get drained by *most* people, let alone teenagers who need constant care, attention and energy.

Now, equipped with more understanding, I'm able to bring my full energy and creative juices to my job and my passions because I'm acutely aware of my introversion tendencies and catch myself before falling. Once I realised that obligatory social situations make me a terrible person to have around – disengaged, scattered, overwhelmed and searching for an immediate exit plan to go home – I stopped doing that to myself and others. Figuring out who I was and what made me tick helped me create alignment, honour my authentic self and only bring the best of P Mami to the table. These days when I feel myself beginning to waver, I know what to do quick smart to recharge my batteries. Get. The. Fuck. Outta. There.

BIG
CREATIVE LIVING
BEYOND FEAR

A WORD, IF I MAY?

Over dinner one night at Chris' house, he asked us all a simple question – as it turned out, another priceless concept gem.

'If you could pick one word to describe yourself or be known for, what would it be? What one word sums up how you want to be seen? Don't answer now – have a think overnight and let me know tomorrow. No answer is the wrong answer.'

I lay awake a long time thinking it through. His question had me stumped; however, I refused to approach the breakfast table the next morning without a thoughtful and considered response. When it came my turn to answer, I replied, 'Warm!'

Everyone nodded. 'Yeah,' I said, 'I like warm things, ya know? I love brown-coloured dogs – they feel warm to me. I love Greek and Italian people because they feel warm to me. I'm attracted to warm colours like orange and yellow and I relax in environments where the climate is warm. Cold people make me feel uncomfortable, but strangers feel like friends if their disposition is warm and sunny.'

Perhaps more than any other advice, Chris' response has stuck with me. 'Okay,' he said. 'Any decision you make moving forward, always choose warm. When you are faced with two choices, if one feels cold and the other feels warm, following warmth will always be the best decision. Choose friends and relationships that feel warm and start to recognise how your body and mind reacts to experiences that come from a place of coldness. If you want to be warm, then choose warm.'

I knew he was right. That simple question and the simple word that arose from it have helped me make countless decisions since.

- When I have dated someone, do they feel warm or do they feel cold?
- When I walk in for a job interview, does the receptionist greet me warmly or are they not interested?
- Do I choose this client or that one?
- Where should I spend my hard-earned money travelling to?

Whenever I am confronted with a decision and find myself trying to determine the best way forward, I simply ask: *which of these options feels warm*? These days, warmth is at the forefront of all the choices I make, both teeny and humungous. I maintain friendships with warm-hearted souls, spend my travels in warmer climates, live in warm-hearted spaces regardless of size, and remove myself from situations where stale energy resides. I will work instantly to remove any cold energy from my business immediately upon feeling or discovering it, as I have learned the hard way how it can negatively impact it on a larger scale. After several hard lessons, I've learned never to ignore my guiding philosophy.

I once hired a chef to work for Pasta Club. Their skillset was unparalleled, so although I found them incredibly cold when we met, I decided to ignore my instinct in favour of their cooking abilities, telling myself they would warm up over time. Over the next few months our customers were well fed, but our staff became increasingly annoyed. Shifts at Pasta Club went from fun, light and enjoyable to hard, mean and disrespectful, reflecting the nature of the new chef. As a direct result, I had several staff resign and an angry blow-up with a customer.

Another time during Plant Mama work, I had only one slot available to do a plant installation, but two businesses interested in working with us, so I arranged meetings with them both. The first was at a three-storey fancy-pants design office where I was given ten minutes to pitch my concept to the managing director. After two minutes of eye contact, she spent the rest of our meeting answering her work emails, and at the end I was told that the budget was for plants, that I'd be given free advertising and connections to their high-level clients for my labour, and also, that they had other plant companies pitching for the job; they'd be in touch if I made it through the first stage.

My second meeting at a tech start-up in Northcote could not have been more different. Waiting to greet me at reception, the owner immediately requested my coffee order and ushered me to flop on the couch and get comfy for our chat. For over an hour we discussed both the plant project and our respective business journeys. Though her budget was below our minimum spend, she had no 'fancy' client connections to dangle, and the scope was less grand than the Melbourne office-design project, she offered me full creative rein and was only comparing one other quote against mine for due diligence.

I took the two potential projects back to our team and we pondered the pros and cons of each. Were client-network opportunities and media exposure more important than collaborating with a smaller client who reflected and embodied our ethos? Was it worth forgoing payment for connections? Which would ultimately be more profitable? All fine questions and important, too, but in the end, it really only boiled down to one decision: which of the two was warm?

The decision to choose Northcote, based upon my key word, provided us a project

filled with warmth, enthusiasm and creativity. Not only was the project a joy, but the Northcote owner ended up providing *countless* network opportunities that have led me to people and companies with a similar vibe to P Mami: warmth.

What I lost from not selecting the Melbourne design job I have gained 30 times over from making a choice based upon my one non-negotiable word. When I lost sight of this and appointed a cold-hearted chef to Pasta Mama, I was quickly reminded of this lesson. Who knew that one of the most important lessons of my life would come from the simple question: 'What is your word?' Choosing a word to guide you in life offers the gift of easy decision making. One word, many choices. So, dare I ask, what is yours?

MAGIC MELINDA

My interest in always seeking blunt and simple honesty for myself means I project the same quality outwards. My community knows they can trust me as I show them my reality, good times and bad. They see the shiny and they see the crap and everything in between: the hard work, the sacrifices, health woes, business struggles and triumphs. I have chosen over the years to speak in times of vulnerability. I have slowly peeled back the mask of perfection and showed up as my chaotic, messy self who is just holding it all together, but somehow still successfully pulling it off.

An indispensable source of wisdom to help me fully embrace my personality has been Magic Melinda. We connect regularly over the phone and throughout my spiritual journey she has been a soul guide in helping me accept my vulnerabilities and become more authentically me. As Magic Melinda once said to me, 'Ohhh pleeease . . . You were never going to come down here unless it was A FANTASTIC LIFE. A big life. A full life. A rockstar journey.'

Oh, Magic Melinda – my spiritual sanity rests in your warm, loving and generous pocket. Magic isn't her first name and I'm sure she'd blush and throw her head back giggling if she knew I called her that, but that's what she is. Legitimate magic, because there is no other way to describe her and what she does in my life and the lives of many others. Even the explanation of her job title is a little mystical. She's part psychic/medium/Universe channeller/reiki healer/herbalist/confidant/therapist and friend with major older-sister vibes. In other words: a light worker.

Out of the four clairs of intuition her two strengths are how she 'hears' (clairaudience) and how she 'knows' through gut feelings or a sixth sense (claircognition). I'm also claircognizant and have clairsentience (touch-sense, like when a chill passes over you). The fourth, clairvoyance, is probably the most well-known and describes a way of 'seeing'. Melinda is my spiritual world tour guide and WHAT A GUIDE TO HAVE FOUND! Honestly. Me and the lucky people who work with her are privy to her truly powerful gifts. She reflects back things we already know deep down, but need a gentle, human voice + an uber calm soul to draw out of us, providing many a-ha moments, the most important being: recognising and accepting our true personality and trust in ourselves.

There is no trickery at play. I'll bet all my future dogs' lives on this, as I have truly felt her positive impact in a multitude of ways. The things she has predicted in bang-on detail with bang-on timelines, the many times she's healed my heart or closed a loop on a situation for me, the random shit she pulls from the sky that blows your mind and brings a tear to the eye, plus the automatic download of wonderful things coming my way (which always come through, by the way). The best part of her appointments is that nothing is ever doomsy or bad; it's always good things, or an explanation for hard things – a pain splain – and I LOVE that.

More than anyone, I think Magic Melinda has taught me, on a PPS (personality, physical, soul) level, how best to use and harness energy. This has always been a gift of mine, but as I've worked with Melinda, it's one I continue to fine-tune.

ENERGY

I know a bit about energy and it's most often the word that others use to describe me. In my media interviews I've been variously described as: 'energetic', 'a ball of energy', 'an energy powerhouse' and 'an energetic whirlwind'. I love that! Because, yes, I take my energy production and expenditure very, very seriously.

This six-letter word has several different dictionary definitions, from 'usable power and effort' to 'fundamental entity of nature transferred between parts of a system in the production of physical change' to 'power as exerted'. You will never find it in an argument between science and religion/spirituality, as both approaches acknowledge its existence and power.

For me, energy lies at the core of my existence. Every single decision, thought and action is based around energy frequency and reception. Energy dictates who I give time to, where I sleep at night, the projects I take on, the people I work with and *every single life action in between*. The ability to see ever-moving energy, be agile and change with it, has profoundly contributed to my work and life success. If I was not aware of my energy or the energy around me, P Mami would cease to exist, I can guarantee you that.

I am hyper aware that others subconsciously read and feel energy (whether they realise it or not), therefore I try to be considerate with what I bring to the room, always asking myself: how are my energy and mood impacting and contributing to this space? My large energy also comes with very intense moods. I have seen, many times, the overwhelming impact that one of my bad moods can have in altering an entire space and people in it. It's *really* full-on. In those moments, my generally positive schmood that operates in flow 85 per cent of the time flips to a psychotic and energy-sucking monster. During those 15 per cent episodes, best make yourself scarce. I try to do the same.

The skill of reading and feeling energy is available to everybody. If you think you are exempt, then think again. The energy is there, no doubt, you just haven't identified it yet. You have been feeling energy shifts all your life, from mundane experiences to high-electric flows.

Have you ever met someone and felt instantly attracted or repelled for no apparent reason? Beyond their looks or words, you 'know' how you feel toward them instinctively. You are feeling their energy vibration against yours; the 'vibe'.

Ever been at a concert where you are dancing like a maniac and losing your mind with the 15,000 other people? The entire crowd feels electric and hypes each other up, contributing to the collective experience – you literally feel a force moving through the crowd and one move can instantly shift the room – hello, Mexican wave. This is energy in high force.

One of the worst feelings in the world is being left in a room with a person you just had a fight or disagreement with. Even after everyone's stopped speaking you can still feel the black mood swirling around. I want to vomit as I type this, just thinking about being in this situation. Your body is tight, you hold your breath, your voice is short and while you would never do it, a cricket bat would be very handy right now. This relates to the phrase 'you can cut the tension with a knife' – that tension we speak of is energy.

Energy in business

Over time, my awareness of energy and consideration of how to use and react to it has become increasingly automatic. Years of consciously learning to read the signals of shifting energy has seen it become easier and require less effort. Intuitively I read the room and take its measure to protect myself and generate the best outcome. Because *energy never lies,* I am able to gather clues as to how people are *really* feeling from their body language, vibe and tone of voice. This has saved me from terrible people and directed me away from stupid business decisions.

The connection between energy and *business,* well now, that's a whole new thing. When something in my business is clearly not working, I know that ultimately, I must make changes to get back in positive flow or alignment. You know that space, when all the elements align and the intention, actions and goals of your life are flying high and running forward at force? When all staff and clients are happy, you are eating right, being social and generally having your passion cup refilled by the day? You definitely know when it's missing, I can vouch for that!

And so do your potential investors and community. See, your flow and energy have an effect on those who enter your orbit. Their interest in connecting with you and your business will come down to how they subconsciously 'feel' around you. An incorrect read, misinterpretation or incorrect alignment of energies can break the success of any relationship or idea. Even the most well-loved people get banished for a momentary lapse and shitty energy. We feel it before we see it.

Managing energy in business is critical, but changes must be carefully considered. Personal life changes can be made faster, with less consideration, more intuition and an element of ease, whereas P Mami has higher stakes. Business decisions must *never* be made based on emotion only, because business can be an emotional rollercoaster ride from hell. In some instances, emotions cannot be trusted.

Reading and using energy

Energy is also a two-way street, right? So, as you absorb the vibez from the homies to the left, you're also sending vibez to the homies on the right. Like attracts like – what you absorb, you emit. SO, EMIT WHAT YOU WANNA ABSORB BECAUSE LIKE ENERGY VIBRATES TOGETHER.

Sadly, it's impossible to forever outrun and escape the 'bad energy' fairies. They show up everywhere, attempting to drain you of everything. Developing the skills to read and assess the flow of energy of people and situations will allow you to make an informed decision as to whether you *accept and absorb* or *redirect* it. By implementing your energy foresight, you may save yourself from some crap life circumstances, so jump onboard.

If you're bamboozled about reading energy and don't know where to start, then let me help you. The strength of this tool is built over time, so please be patient. As you begin to repel and redirect what's not good for you, the right things will have space to show up. Positive energy attracts positive energy. The more bad energy you block and redirect, the more room there is for GOOD THINGS to seep in.

Start small by trying to notice subtle shifts or changes between you and others, or within spaces. The easiest, most practical way to begin understanding and assessing energy is to consider how you feel after spending time with a particular person. Are they an energy giver or an energy sucker – do you feel better and 'filled up' when you leave them or do you feel drained and exhausted? Did they give you energy, take your energy, or do you feel the same as you did before you saw them? Granted, everyone has terrible days and energies can be low for us all, so just consider how they make you feel *most* of the time.

As you begin to develop your energy-reading and -using ability, you might find these directions helpful. Try to mindfully practise one each time you're with another person and over time they will become instinctive.

- Notice if your body reacts to this person. I normally feel my stomach flip or shivers down my spine if something is off.
- Assess the other's body language. Are their limbs crossed and closed off or are they open and relaxed?
- How close are you standing to them? People naturally give off an aura. Your body will

As you begin to repel and redirect what's not good for you, the right things will have space to show up. Positive energy attracts positive energy. The more bad energy you block and redirect, the more room there is for GOOD THINGS to seep in.

instinctively feel drawn closer or repelled.

- What is your heart doing? Is it racing and are you anxious during this moment, or do you feel relaxed and at ease?
- Notice how they speak about other people. If they spend most of their time talking poorly of others, then that's probably how they will speak about you.
- Eye contact will tell you a lot about whether your energy connection makes them uncomfortable or comfortable, alerting you to alignment or non-alignment.
- Observe their expressions as they speak. If they wince when a specific topic is brought up, something is vibrating differently around that.
- Notice their presence and energy. Are they excitable, grounded, considered, darty, talkative, etc? How does that fit with you?
- Identify how others behave around them. How do they react to and treat them? Use others' subconscious tools to provide you with subtle hints.

Protecting your energy

Understanding how you cultivate your best, fully charged, high-energy self will revolutionise your personal relationships. Learning to erect boundaries to protect your crucial recharge time will ensure you arrive at every human interaction with a full mind, heart, soul and energy field, giving you the strength and power to tackle whatever is presented. I regularly implement boundaries to support my energy refill time. These include:

- Working independently alongside others who complement my skills.
- Avoiding dinner reservations on weekdays as I am too tired from work.
- Taking three days after each Pasta Club to recharge. That goes for any other high-energy activity, too, such as making podcasts.
- Not travelling with extroverts for longer than a weekend (unless they are respectful of my needs).
- Spending Sundays (where possible) alone to self-care and prepare for the week ahead.
- Leaving a social gathering or event the moment I feel drained.
- Spending as much time as possible in nature, preferably alone, to recalibrate.
- Making time for idle art and doodling.
- Not going to an event if I am not excited to see anyone.
- Instantly cutting ties with energy suckers.

To experience a human relationship cultivated through the exchange of good intentional energy may be one of life's sweetest activities for the taking. Energy reading can both save your arse at any given moment and provide you with the skills to effectively allow *only* good energy in. From here on in, start to notice and play with subtle differences in energy. As you begin to work with your body's natural ability as an energy producer, radar and blocker, start to adapt how you project and absorb energy and observe the difference it makes.

Most importantly, though, is learning to understand yourself. Developing your PPS – Personality, Physicality and Soul – is time well spent and never wasted. Learning how your personality works with others' will take you to the next level.

Although we didn't have time to go into them here, some other super-useful concepts that did not make an appearance at today's show include: your Life Path Number, Ayurveda, the Myers-Briggs Type Indicator, DiSC and Gretchen Rubin's Four Tendencies framework. Yes, I know that sounds like a chaotic mix-bag of approaches – welcome to the wonderful world of P Mami!

Whether with these or with other learnings, any time spent getting to know yourself and how you best operate in the world will be invaluable. At times it may feel frustrating and nonsensical, but doing the work will pay dividends. Stay hydrated, take plenty of breaks, laugh out loud and top up with snacks – our life journey is long but worth every step. From one energetic, hyperactive and on fire human to another, *you've got this*.

Any time spent getting to know yourself and how you best operate in the world will be invaluable.

PRINCIPLE 4
Personality

Our unique personality brings diversity and joy to the world. Learn what makes you distinctive and celebrate it.

Energy never lies. Follow what feels good and avoid what feels off. When you redirect the things that are not good for you, it will create space for the right things show up.

Becoming your authentic self is the by-product of the work you undertake to fully know thyself and will unlock your abundant creativity.

Ask yourself

What parts of your life replenish your energy source and allow your personality traits to shine, baby, shine?

Do you clearly know what your personal strengths and weaknesses are and how they are best used or delegated?

Where do you sit on the extrovert/introvert spectrum? Do you create environments that protect your boundaries and recharge your spirit?

What is your word? (Hint: warm, interested, chutzpah, bright . . .)

Can you pay closer attention to how your inner energy vibes with the outer world and make adjustments that work in your favour?

chapter five

PEOPLE

CAN'T LIVE WITH 'EM, CAN'T LIVE WITHOUT 'EM

My relationship with human beings is an interesting one. I can say wholeheartedly, I would rather be with dogs above people! But, I cannot deny that the latter have taught me more in life. Some people will fade out of your memory over time and some will last forever, as if they are an extra limb or organ in your body. Some souls will breathe creativity, life force and wonderment into your life while others will cause you enough stress to reconsider your very existence here – and somewhere between those two is everybody else. Our fellow humans are our biggest teachers as we learn to see and relate to one another with empathy while remaining loyal to our inner voice.

Leaping into action instead of giving in to a meltdown is the quickest way to find a solution;

energy matches movement, not stagnation.

TABLECLOTHS

This life I'm living is a dream – until it isn't. People hire me for my colour, creativity and fun chaotic energy, which is gold most of the time. *Sometimes* not so much. Learning how to trust others to support me as they operate in their own lane of genius has been a game-changer.

It's Friday night and I'm chilling with a margarita, casually flinging things into a suitcase in prep for Sunday's flight – how organised am I? – when the client texts: *What time is your team arriving in the morning to set the tables?*

I reply immediately. *Planning to set them myself before my appearance. I have all the tablecloths with me (in Melbourne) and am bringing them Sunday??*

Nerve-wracking dots fill my screen. Then: *Oh?! Sorry – no – we need them set all weekend. Those tables need to be ready by 11 am tomorrow!*

MY BRAIN EXPLODES as my shaking fingers dial her number. As soon as she picks up, I launch straight in. 'Hey, it's me. So sorry for the confusion. That's fine . . . no worries! I'll figure it out, we always do . . .'

Stony silence. I get the feeling she doesn't believe me.

'Honestly, don't stress,' I say, as breezily as I can. 'I always find a way to sort these things out. Leave it with me and I'll get back to you with a plan shortly.'

FFFFUUUUUUUUCCCCCCCK! Now, you know me by now. Of course, I trust in the Universe, but . . . How the fuck am I supposed to get the tablecloths interstate overnight – also find flowers, plus produce, AND get someone to set everything up in another state in the next 12 hours? I look at my watch. It's 5:30 pm Friday. Stunning.

Thankfully, the client is equally invested. We hit up all our contacts and between us manage to locate someone flying from Melbourne to Adelaide later that night who can take the tablecloths with them. First step, done. Next: produce, flowers and styling. My Instagram community *never* fails me, so I put out a call for help. Responses flood in, among them the uber lovely, helpful small-business florist Lucy who (yay!) also has contacts in produce. Willing to throw her weekend plans aside to help a panicked P Mami, Lucy offers to get to the Adelaide Flower Market by 4 am Saturday, collect several kilos of produce, then take them all to the venue to set up and style the tables, promising to have them done by 11 am. Though I haven't seen any of Lucy's styling work, my gut says 'trust', so I do. Next day she texts me just before 11 am. *Done.*

When I arrive on Sunday, I immediately see that Lucy has done a better job with the tables than my panicked self ever could have in a stressed-out state. We bond over cocktails and Pasta Mama plates, dancing alongside a tentful of happy patrons. The client is grinning from ear to ear. 'This is better than we ever imagined,' she says.

IT'S ALL ABOUT THE PEOPLE, PEOPLE

What could have been a huge error and problem ultimately delivered a better outcome than the one initially planned for. Why? It taught me an invaluable lesson and reminded me to trust in others. People don't realise that most of the time when you ask for help in a meaningful way, others will turn up for you. Especially when it's paid work. People save the day sometimes and, on those days, people truly are the best!

Many times, I have put myself out there to help others believing that eventually, what you put out you will receive back tenfold. That is the P Mami secret to success.

Alongside asking with intention, I hold an unswerving belief that, 'We'll figure it out, we always do.' I often lean on blind trust that the outcome will serve my faith. Okay, I admit, around 3 per cent of me thinks maybe it won't work out, but I hold unshakably onto a 97-per-cent belief that it will, because: like energy attracts like energy. The tablecloths *had* to arrive in Adelaide and someone else *had* to do the work because I was not available until Sunday.

I trusted we could solve this problem and then worked to make it happen, because solutions don't come knocking on your door, you go knocking on theirs. Calmly hanging up the phone and leaping into action instead of giving in to a meltdown is the quickest way to find a solution; energy matches movement, not stagnation. Most importantly, I had to trust my intuition. Lucy's name stuck out among the long list of others and choosing her was the right move to pull off this miracle. As discussed in the previous chapter, energy exchange is the key to solid relationships, even between strangers. Good people attract good people; good energy attracts good energy. On this basis, I handed over a big project to a stranger whom I'd never met, who ultimately did a wonderful job – better than I could have done in that moment.

I like to think of energy as karma, too. Many times, I have put myself out there to help others, believing that eventually, what you put out you will receive back tenfold. *That* is the P Mami secret to success. So then, let's look at a few different types of people, because relationships are key to everything.

TEACHERS

> Better than a thousand days of diligent study is one day with a great teacher.
>
> – Japanese proverb

We all need just one to change our lives. Mine was Mrs Fox.

Mrs Fox was tall with short brown hair, a friendly-but-soft nature and kind eyes. She rushed everywhere, but somehow made it look as though she were gracefully gliding over the carpet, and busy as she was, always made time for her students.

It was Year 10 and sometime during the year everyone in the grade was required to take 'Media' as a subject, which I was dreading as I assumed that meant learning about newspapers and magazines – vomit, vomit, vomit to my 15-year-old brain. The media classroom was in this weird little nook between stair levels, so I was bored and unimpressed until Mrs Fox welcomed us with a warm, friendly smile and introduced the term's topic: photography, or what she called 'drawing with light'.

Though I had a total of ZERO experience other than taking random holiday snaps, this sounded like something I could get interested in. Over the next few months, we learned manual photography from the ground up, including our first lesson that day: how to roll the film off the canister into the camera body without exposing it to daylight and wrecking it. Homework was *very thoughtfully* capturing 20 images – no digital snap-happy Harrys back then. Once you'd taken your shots, you'd head into the dark room and shove your negatives under a little light-exposure machine and begin the very slow process of testing and developing under different light exposures. Once happy, you'd fix your print in chemicals, peg it up to dry, and eventually have a photographic print.

Sometimes I spent all week producing just one photograph, a task that required meticulous fine motor skills alongside supreme patience – usually my ultimate circle of hell. However, for some unknown reason, the opposite occurred. By the second week I was fully excited to attend each class and learn more. Media class became the best fifty minutes of my day – I'd finally found something to channel my chaotic energy into: intentional creative expression.

This art form took over my life which, to be honest, I welcomed. I was at that age where I felt alienated by everything: my parents did not understand me, my friend groups were not the right fit, school was boring, and it felt like each day was 88 hours long. So I became dedicated to my newfound passion. I kept a yellow A5 book and a pencil sitting on my bedside table in which to record the endless ideas I had for photographs. I'd wake in the middle of the night and write down: 'boy and dog in bubble bath, lots of bubbles' or 'Nana and Grandad living-room chairs holding hands' – images capturing simple-but-special moments of connection.

My fellow classmates submitted a few images each week, but I ploughed full-steam ahead, spitting out anywhere between 10 and 20 photographs a week. (One of my early photographs is on the next page.) Any spare moment I had was consumed with taking photos or developing them. I gave up all my lunchtimes and did not care when Mum would scream at me for ruining my third school dress with darkroom chemicals. I was executing my highest (and first) form of true creative expression and obsession, one of life's most wonderful gifts.

From the first lesson, Mrs Fox saw my interest spark. My eagerness to learn every inch, nook and cranny of photography was abundantly clear, and since nothing drives the interest of a teacher more than a student willing to learn, Mrs Fox and I were a match made in heaven. Well, on that front at least. Outside our common interest in photography, I can confidently say that Mrs Fox and I were on completely different ends of the personality spectrum. I would dart from one topic to the next, asking a second question halfway through my first question. I was disorganised, continuously moved around the classroom and forgot to bring *most* things to class, arriving *drenched* in food stains 98 per cent of the time. Mrs Fox, on the other hand, was the calmest person I had ever met, softly spoken, thoughtful yet direct, and always patiently waited for me to finish my tangent. I felt grounded in her presence.

> In life we are forever students, forever learning, so the chances of you finding an inspiring teacher are both highly likely and highly plausible.

We were complete opposites: my darty energy, laser-focused enthusiasm and blind talent for taking photos were grounded by Mrs Fox's warmth, knowledge and patience. Instead of forcing her opinion on me, she would gently suggest trying different exposures, or to consider what impact taking an extra step backward may have had on my picture. (THIS is key, folks: always ask a developing creative about *the process* rather than passing judgement on their final product. Creativity is linked to our freedom of expression and if our expression is considered 'wrong' compared to arbitrary standards, we inherently think *we* are wrong, so PLEASE be careful.)

We had a beautiful connection and I now seek this balanced combination in all my working relationships – a successful life recipe. This relationship and its birthing of my first creative outlet helped me realise the impact that one person can have on your ability to absorb a new lesson or enjoy a new experience. Mrs Fox identified my all-consuming delight in photography and gifted me her time and knowledge, helping me become the creative entrepreneur I am today. To learn at 15 years old that no creative way is incorrect, and that anything can easily 'be adjusted', is undeniably priceless.

I hope you've had your own Mrs Fox, but if not yet, please believe – it ain't over 'til it's over! In life, we are forever students, forever learning, so the chances of you finding an inspiring teacher are both highly likely and highly plausible. Education degree or not, there are people all around you sharing already – so keep your eyes and ears open to seeing them, and then just ask: 'Please, show me your ways.'

LA FAMIGLIA

Oh families. Both infuriating and lovely, they will challenge your authentic self *the most*. Every day, people are giving their true selves away to fulfil their family's expectations. At one point, I was one of them.

Mine is a fairly typical family dynamic – two annoying-but-loving parents and an older brother who is both the opposite of me and also the same. Cam and I are both stubborn, creative, funny and passionate about going *against* the status quo, but also sit on very different sides of the fence on many things – oh man, the fights. In the end, we figure things out because our parents raised us as a unit: 'four as one'.

My deep love for my grandparents is beyond what my soul can communicate. The older generations stir something inside of me so, of course, the ones in my family are just . . . beyond. I wrote my nana Audrey and her sister Gladys a letter each before they passed away, describing the qualities they had gifted me, alongside all the reasons I loved them and a full list of their iconic family dishes. Our elders need to hear from us more and receive our recognition that we see and appreciate them. Our lives trace back to their decisions; whether in favour or not, they're part of us.

And my parents . . . can't live with 'em, can't live without 'em. The thing is, parents are annoying and I don't think my parents are the only ones, it's legit *all* of them. I used to think that Goldie Hawn would be THE BEST and most fun parent EVER until I saw an interview with her and her daughter, Kate Hudson. Kate was describing all of the annoying 'mum' things Goldie does . . . the list was looong. So, even the 'funnest' mum in the world is part of that crew. Yet, despite their irritating moments, I love my parents intensely. I know how lucky I am.

As I've got older, I've learned a thing or two about family dynamics. One is that you and your parents were partnered to teach each other things. The second is that you cannot be *too* angry at your parents for their choices, because most of the time *they have no idea what they are doing!* Most parents are just trying their best with what they have. They take what they learned from their parents, add a grab-bag of knowledge and societal expectations, sprinkle it with *their own stresses* and just try to keep their little humans alive. When you remove the parent mask from your folks' faces, you will see that they are just people with their own triggers, fears, inner-child workings and tendencies, much like yourself, and the only way to move forward together is with empathy and openness. Personally, I find the empathy part much easier than the open part, but this is something I'm working on.

Sometimes, within family and generational cycles, there comes a soul destined to shake things up, bring a cycle to its close and initiate a new way. These tadpoles will always meet resistance as they are changing the way things have 'always been done' and some family members find this offensive. Take heart if this little wriggler is you. In the end, you must honour yourself. Everyone is responsible for their own life. We need wild tornadoes to break family cycles and the Holmes version in this lifetime is . . . me.

Truth is, if I had listened to my parents then there would be no Plant Mama or P Mami, no book in your hands nor the wonderful life I live. Of course, with due reflection I have come to understand that they were never *consciously* blocking my path forward, but simply honouring their parental role to ensure my security and survival using the tools they'd been taught. Parents just want their kids to be safe which can sometimes blur how they see their kids' happiness, as if security is more important than fulfilment. I mean, it's pretty common to assume the security of a predictable income or secure job is what's best. I'm just not suited to that kind of life.

Over time, as they've witnessed my growing success, Ma and Pa Holmes have come to understand the P Mami pleasure perspective. At least 50 per cent of them wants me to follow my happiness and fulfilment and the other 50 per cent of them will always worry. Based on their own past family expectations and societal cues, they are anxious about what I am sacrificing for P Mami and that it won't pay off.

My parents and I have had many hard confrontations over my life decisions and new beliefs. Each time, I brace myself for the inevitable emotional explosion, yet in the end we survive. As I become more myself and they continue to love me regardless, we forge a new, stronger relationship and P Mami grows from strength to strength. If I had listened to my parents and followed their orders and expectations, I would truly have missed out on some of the most wonderful life experiences, the ones that come from doing the unruly things that stir in you, despite going against what you have been raised to believe.

For all of us, a major lesson is to discover and learn to differentiate between the two voices in our head: the one created by your parents or guardians, and the one born in us. Empathy will help us understand our parents, but that shouldn't stop us forging our own path, even if that means walking away for a bit while you try to work things out for yourself. Living in the world free from others' expectations will help you hear your inner voice.

LOVERS

The most isolating feeling in the world is to lose your authentic self to romantic love. How can something feel so nice, but at the same time separate us from who we are? Sometimes we change as people while we are in relationships and become afraid to share our new thoughts, as if we are meant to stagnate in our past. So, instead of disrupting our lives we slowly dissolve ourselves to keep the peace, becoming ill in the process.

I remember a moment in my Richmond bedroom about six months after my first real hard-core heartbreak. Looking around the room, I noticed everything was white. White furniture, white bed sheets, white photo frames – there was no colour anywhere. I checked my wardrobe and all my clothes were white, black, grey or denim. Not an inch of colour. Before dating this person, I had *only* worn colour and my past bedrooms had been filled with patterns and plants and THINGS. Before we'd dated, I'd worn bright yellow pants with blue shoes, not plain white t-shirts and skinny black jeans with black ankle boots. I started wearing those things because *he* was attracted to that style.

He never asked me to dress like that nor asked me to design my room all white, but I did anyway – to make him happy. To make him find me more attractive. I relinquished myself and my style for a love that didn't appreciate my authentic self – maybe because even *I* didn't trust her yet. When we broke up, I realised I had spent every afternoon waiting for him to finish work so I could ask what he wanted for dinner. WHY WAS I NOT ASKING MYSELF WHAT *I* WANTED FOR DINNER? I desired this relationship *so much* I was willing to sacrifice myself to keep it going.

Uneasy and confused by the person I was trying to become for love, I torched every other aspect of myself only to realise that in losing myself, I lost the relationship. Through therapy I learned that the purpose of these connections in our lives is to remind us that love *never* asks you to show up as anything else but your full authentic self. I mean, listen, that same guy used to mock my music choices and now *thousands* of followers like my playlists . . . so clearly, that relationship was never meant to be. On the other hand, I have seen the most wonderful relationships born and move fruitfully through *decades* because both parties support the other's true self and need to change and grow. An authentic partnership is one of the most meaningful and impactful connections we can make – unconditional love and authenticity radiate even to those outside its orbit.

My white bedroom moment was the beginning of my journey to an authentic self. As I began to drag plants, coloured doonas, Turkish rugs and blue-velvet pantsuits back into my life, I felt myself slowly reappearing. After a long and anxious time indoors repairing my little heart, I finally clambered back into the world and began reinvigorating my life with the things that made *me* happy, like eating plain eggs for dinner and wearing paint-splattered overalls in public. Plant Mama was born because I had extra time and focus. As she grew, I felt people accepting the real me which encouraged me to go further. Same with Pasta Mama. I've been more genuine in her realm from the get-go because I've experienced the power of vulnerability and authenticity.

I will die on the hill alone before I sacrifice the efforts I've made to cultivate my unique self. We all deserve to be around people who accept every part of us – our 'crappy' playlists, the way we slice tomatoes, our tuneless singing and our favourite shoes. It's also okay for these to change over time. You do not have to wear blue Crocs forever, okay, but for right now, they're cool. When we expose ourselves fully to the right people, the ones who let us be ourselves, we access what it means to live fully. The right life to live, I say.

FRIENDS

> I see true friends as crucial to our life journey. When they turn up at the right time during the wrong time for you, the world shifts.

I have great friendships now, but for most of my life I was alone – by choice. During school and even at university, I felt different to everyone else. I could make connections with people easily enough, but never in a way that felt natural to who I was. Every so often I would collect a special gem, and those mates are still here for the ride, but mostly I felt off-ish vibes with every group I met – none of them were for me.

It wasn't until moving to Melbourne at age 24 and the birth of Plant Mama that my true friends began to show up in random and coincidental ways. As I began honouring my true self, my life's greatest friends came out to play, beckoning P Mami forth. Like energy, friendships are a two-way street. While we all dance differently, finding a person willing to learn your moves and teach you theirs makes the whole dang trip worthwhile.

We all have what I like to call our GST – our 10 per cent annoying quality – the thing you put up with in your friends because no one arrived to this world unflawed. Mine is that I won't answer a text message about a simple coffee date for six months, but if you call me in the middle of my speech at Beyoncé's wedding needing a mental-health hype up, I'll be outta that wedding in a shot and right by your side. I am terrible as a weekly-organised-walks friend but shine in a crisis – not just for you, but anyone you love too.

I had once not spoken to a friend for a solid two years (just out of general forgetfulness, not lack of love!) and she randomly called, telling me her mother had passed away that morning. I was on the next plane and stayed with her for the following three weeks, not because I could afford time off work (quite the opposite, actually), but because there's nothing more important than helping a sister in need. Just know this . . . I will show up when the chips are down, no matter what, even if I'm hopeless at any sort of regular coffee-date arrangements.

Friendships are about playing a constant game of see-saw that results in laughter, screams, tears and joy. Sometimes one person needs to be lifted high for a period while the other shouts encouragingly from below – and then the wind changes and your positions flip. Other times you're balanced in the middle, heads backs, hyena-laughing. Just find the peeps you want on the ride with you. The friendship GST is well worth paying to experience the 90 per cent goodness we receive from our friends and the pleasure of having them beside you.

Your true tribe will show up for you when you show up for yourself.

Authentic friendships can honestly save your life, I really mean that. When your parents fail to understand, your boss is toxic and your partner is being a fuckhead, your friends will always be there. Like Epicurus, I see true friends as crucial to our life journey. When they turn up at the right time during the wrong time for you, the world shifts. To attract these people in your life, you must be that friend to others – honest, supportive, helpful. And most of all, vulnerable. As I have revealed my shameful quirks with honesty, my friends have rallied to support me. I have survived this life *because of them.* Even when I don't ask for help, they turn up and carry me through whatever saga I have found myself in.

The more I come into my authentic self, the wider the network of people I connect with. Through bringing the real P Mami to work, many of my client contacts have become wonderful friends. Beyond anything, this is probably the most valuable thing that has come from owning my own company – the people I've collected along the way. Most especially, the long list of badass women excelling hard out in their careers. It's incredibly inspiring to call these people mates as we lean on and build each other up.

Your true tribe will show up for you when you show up for yourself . Watch your life transform as you work toward authentic connections only. No settling of self found here, thank you!

SPROUT – BETTER TOGETHER

Not all companions have to be people. In fact, my favourites are the furry kind. I had pined for my own personal doggo companion my *entire adult life*, but also knew that waiting until I could be a proper dog parent was the responsible thing to do. In the meantime, I dog-sat everyone else's hounds and often went to the puppy park so I could pat other dogs to fulfil my canine needs.

While home for Christmas in 2018 I visited my friend's parents' breeding kennels. A young border collie called Pip came to me immediately and would not leave my side. We instantly fell in love and my friend's dad, Gary, offered me her, but I wasn't ready. When I visited again Pip was still there, so I asked if I could take her, but by then, Gary had other plans. He had decided to keep and breed her the following year.

I messaged Gary in August: *Hey Gary, if Pip has any puppies, let me know as I am interested!*

He responded straight away: *She just had a litter this morning.*

Li'l Sprout arrived eight weeks later into my hands and heart. We're unbreakable partners in dopamine crime, hyperactive teammates, sensory squirrels and inattentive lightbulbs together. Without Sprout, my mental and physical health

would epically fail. She has helped settle so much of my ADHD as I have to be routined and organised with her – daily walks, staying on top of her food and giving her tick medication. She is 100 per cent present with me – not on a phone like a human companion might be or complaining about her shitty day; the extra heartbeat in the quiet room that would otherwise sometimes feel lonely, the funny friend with charisma who always makes me laugh. When I am sick, she lies on the unwell part of my body and she always hoovers up my scattered crumbs.

She'll show me instantly who should not be trusted and her bark is able to alert me if something is off in the energy. When she feels me stressing at the desk she'll leap onto my lap, using her weight to calm and ground me, to pull me out of my head. When I am crying, she'll lick the tears from my face then sleep with her head on my heart all night, as if to repair me. In social situations where I feel overwhelmed and anxious, she acts like a buffer gifting me two things: 1) a great conversation starter; and 2) a cute barrier (who loves pats) between me and everyone else. If I need to burn some extra energy or run around, Sprout is always free, available and willing to join the party. I can count on her to be my ultimate hype queen, always.

Obviously, getting a dog, *especially* a hyperactive dog like a border collie, is a huge responsibility and not one to be taken lightly. Please don't get a dog unless you can, not just keep it alive, but give it the *best life* possible – there is good karma in treating your animals well. For me, my little pal Sprout has truly provided me with a second wind for life and is a stunning dopamine hitter. The perfect-sized companion, she supports me in quiet ways as she shows up without fail, exchanging pure love and cuddles for bones, walks and games. By far, Sprout offers the easiest exchange for the most support. Always better when together.

THE 'I' IN COMMUNITY

As popular wisdom says: you're the average of the five people you spend the most time with. Or my absolute favourite: if you lie down with dogs, you'll wake up with fleas. So, choose whom you spend your time with wisely. The people around you will affect your ability to show up as your multi-layered self. Sometimes you are unable to choose those groups – like family or work colleagues – but luckily, friends and romantic relationships balance that out.

Each offers different things over your lifetime. Your family is here to teach you, your friends to support you, romantic relationships to extend you, and work relationships to force you to grow in multiple ways through acceptance and tolerance. You will spend a large portion of your time among a variety of personalities within these groups, which will affect your ability to be your authentic self. Of course, I encourage you to decisively cut any ties with anyone who disrupts your true sense of self or dims the light in you by making you feel smaller.

Unfortunately, there are some groups that can never be fully avoided. In these instances, it's even more important to cultivate the skills and courage to show up as the 'real' you, no matter the difficulty. This becomes easier as we learn to prioritise our inner voice over the noise coming from others. Their voices must be quietened in order to hear the one inside that's quietly stomping about asking you to change, to seek, to be.

How do we shush those external voices, you ask? Well first, start literally: by getting quiet. Go find a comfortable place on the floor at home or wherever you are, taking a notepad and pen with you. Ask yourself the following questions and close your eyes as you wait silently to hear or feel the answer, then write it down.

- **What do I want to do with my time every day – what does an 'average-but-delightful' day look like and what does a 'magnificent' day look like?**
- **Which activities have I done over the past 12 months that made me stand taller? Big or small, serious or casual – ANYTHING.**
- **What resource do I feel depleted of and what's the first place I think of when I look to restore and recharge it?**

Once you write your answers and see what comes up, you'll be able to draw the line between what others are saying or wanting you to do, and what your inner voice is telling you. Once you've determined what it is you need to make you happy, then it's time to go about making it happen. But how?

It all boils down to this, my pretty little petunias: we must learn to gather around us people who reflect and encourage our desired self. They will fill us up with their love, as we will do in return, elevating us through life's muckiness. Still, at times we will inevitably be served their opposites: the drainers. It's unfortunate but true that *these* people somehow teach us the big whoppers, building our strongest selves through their home-run lessons. Those times are hard, but through them we will grow stronger. Through the pain they inflict we learn to love and nurture our chosen ones. Their lessons teach us to recognise the true gift of a fellow traveller.

Through it all *you* are the captain of your ship and must trust thyself to steer thyself. But, since I haven't seen any large ships running as one-man bands, you must also locate and gather your shipmates. Connect or live a lonely life. Ultimately, all we really need to survive is the support of a few decent mates. Gather your people, people, because in the end, they are all we have.

PRINCIPLE 5
People

To have and be a good friend is life's greatest gift. Show up as both giver and receiver, accepting friendship's GST.

What you put out you'll receive back tenfold. Be a jerk and receive jerks throughout your days. Be hardworking and open and you'll gather an army of supportive mates.

The most valuable thing to gain in this lifetime are the people you collect along the way. Keep the ones who light you up and drop any who make you feel smaller. Period.

Share yourself openly and the right tribe will show up to honour, embrace and support you.

Ask yourself

Do you open yourself to people that transit your life for a season, reason or lifetime?

Do you put your hand out to help others? When you ask for help, who lends you theirs?

What is the greatest lesson that a life teacher has taught you about yourself and the world? (Hint: this could be a schoolteacher, family member, friend, co-worker or lover.)

Does your current relationship make you feel like you're stuck wearing a life-sucking, all-white wardrobe? If so, RUN!

What GST do you bring to your friends? What is theirs? How can you make more space to accept each other?

chapter six

POWER

YOUR UNIQUENESS IS YOUR GIFT, THE SOURCE OF YOUR POWER

A person in their power displays growth, assertiveness, vulnerability, clarity, empathy and an awareness and application of their unique gifts. It's rarely owned by the loudest or richest person in the room, often it's the quietest and poorest who have the most strength. But true power is only available if one is willing to do the work. See, it's a regenerative resource: the more you use it for positive things, the more it grows and expands. Power is energy at its highest vibration. Mastering and understanding yourself is the quickest way to locate its inner force within you. It exists irrespective of whether you use it or not – and if you don't use it, you are missing out on some seriously *powerful* and *magnificent magic juju* that is yours for the taking.

SILENCE
THE NOISE.
SEE THE
PATH.

NOT BROKEN

For a long time, despite all the work I'd done on myself, I still felt as if a part of me were broken. My chaotic colourful ways didn't fit the typical business approach and I was always dropping and breaking things, including myself. Sometimes, you find your power where you least expect it.

It's 7 am on a Monday in 2019 and I am executing my classic morning routine. I head down to the local café carrying my laptop and set up at a corner table where I plan to punch through work tasks and admin. On this particular morning, as I do a few times a year when Plant Mama becomes overtly hectic and needs some *hardcore* computer work to pull her into line, I take some Ritalin I got from a friend.

I sit down without ordering, so the waitress comes over to check on me, asking if I'd like my usual. I blurt, 'Oh no thanks, I just took Ritalin, so I need to wait a bit for coffee!'

'Of course. You have ADHD!' she replies.

I'm taken aback. 'Oh, umm, no, I just got it from a friend. But, maybe? I don't know?' I am feeling very awkward at this point, as if I've suddenly been exposed.

'Ha,' she says. 'I've actually been meaning to bring this up with you . . . I have watched you every morning for the past few months and you do so many similar things to me that are like my ADHD. You don't sit for longer than 10 minutes without getting up from the table or making a call, you can have seven tangential conversations going at once and have lots of high energy. I just noticed how you were doing things and thought I'd mention it because it really helped me once I knew. My girlfriend used to get so frustrated that I'd never listen to her and forget everything, so I had to get on top of it.'

The world feels like it stops turning, as if my life has exploded before me.

She clocks my dumbfounded state. 'I have a break in about an hour if you want to talk more?' she offers.

'Sure,' I nod.

I close all my workbooks and push them aside, clearing space for my world to unfold. Then I type into Google's search: Symptoms of ADHD. For the next 30 minutes I scroll several reputable sites. I check off every item on every single symptom list. *Every single box*! This throwaway comment from a slight acquaintance has resolved my entire 29-confusing-years-on-the-planet conundrum. I close my laptop and look out the window. My eyes blur. Maybe there is *not* something wrong with me after all? Maybe *this* is the answer rather than a human malfunction or flaw. Is the only thing wrong with me that I *thought* something was wrong with me? . . .
Maybe I am NOT BROKEN!

TIME PRESSURE
WEBSITE
Art
only
in this
book
No
allowe

UNIQUE GIFTS AND TORNADO SWITCHES

For most of my life I have felt like a strange character, as if I don't really fit in anywhere, and while this caused some level of stress and unrest when I was a teenager, I am genuinely okay with it now and, in fact, celebrate it. When answering the classic interview question, 'What would you tell your younger self?' my answer has never wavered. P Mami's advice for little J is: *It's okay to be different. Your uniqueness will be your greatest life asset, so don't block, settle or change it for anyone or anything.*

Despite the strong inner voice that told me I wanted to be different, I tried to hide my individuality for so many years in fear of tribe rejection, worried that showing my messy, chaotic and true self would turn people away. So instead, I struggled tirelessly to uphold societal and family expectations only to become bored, unfulfilled, moody and lost. As the Universe nudged me, I slowly mustered the courage to start speaking up for myself and begin showing up as the 'real' me: all of me, all the time, with all my layers, feelings and thoughts. I learned, often the hard way, that to *connect* we need to be *relatable* to people. That's how trust is built.

In the café in Collingwood, during the waitress's break, I showered her with questions, unable to keep up with my racing thoughts and overwhelmed by how similar our experiences sounded. As she went back to slinging coffee, my intuition told me to cancel my week ahead and push all my plant installations and meetings to the following week. Instinctively I knew I needed time and space to throw myself down the rabbit hole and toward a space of healing. I had already spent so much of my life trying to figure out *what it was* that made my life so hard and different from everyone else's – this could be the key. A week of work could be sacrificed for finally receiving the manual to my brain to unlock my self-mystery. Maybe it would even open the door that kept all my shameful feelings inside and hidden away from others.

I learned, often the hard way, that to connect we need to be relatable to people. That's how trust is built.

I absorbed everything in my reach, ordering and reading all the books, walking for *days* as I listened to podcasts and audiobooks, watching documentaries until 2 am and finding helpful Instagram accounts filled with tips and statistics. My obsession granted me freedom from the negative thoughts and energies I had constantly heaped on myself, marking my struggles as a personality flaw, not a biological disorder. All my life I had felt as if everyone else in the world knew what was going on and how to adult, and I that had missed that class because I was off with the creative fairies.

After my week down the hole (a classic ADHD thing to do, I now know!), I emerged with a plethora of information and was open, willing and ready to find a solution. My GP referred me to a specialist ADHD psychiatrist for diagnostic tests. Within 5 minutes of our meeting the psychiatrist felt confident I had come to the right place, simply because of my inability to *sit still* in the chair, my high-energy nature and flighty attention – all strong signals of ADHD. The test results confirmed it.

ADHD used to be called attention deficit disorder (ADD) and was commonly used to describe those boys in the classroom who could never sit still and constantly interrupted. The understanding of it as a condition was expanded in 1987 when 'H' for hyperactivity was added, to become ADHD. It has been variously described as: a mental disorder, psychological condition, neurodevelopmental disorder and a mental health disorder and presents on a spectrum that encompasses three broad states: 1. Predominantly hyperactive, 2. Predominantly inattentive, 3. Combined both.

Moi? I have been graced with having the 'combined both' type, meaning I can neither sit still nor listen to anything boring.

Since my diagnosis, my psychiatrist and I have worked together using strategies and medications to help manage my condition. In addition to the pharmaceuticals prescribed, I've trialled other less traditional practices. Bullet journals, time-management alarms, the ADHD coach, specific food groups, physical therapy – I've tried them all in an attempt to harness this wild gift and some of them have helped.

The road to getting diagnosed in Australia is sadly very long and expensive and I understand the privilege I've had in accessing these appointments. I hear how difficult it is for others waiting in line for help. It's heartbreaking and frustrating because when any neurodivergent soul is given the space and the support to be themselves, geniuses are born and have the capacity to build the world with their innovation and energy.

For those of us with ADHD, we can try to learn everything possible, go to every ADHD specialist available to us and take every type of prescription pill out there in order to help, but ultimately, I believe that locating our tornado switch is the answer: the thing that flicks us into gear and pushes us forward into our lane of genius, toward our soul's purpose.

If we neurodivergent folk can locate what is of interest to us and are supported to go after it, we can not only obtain what we are focusing on, but we *excel* at it. Interest provides dopamine and dopamine provides energy and focus. By the way, that tornado switch is not only found in ADHD folk – everyone has a curiosity button. If you stay alert, you'll feel an electric force when it flicks on, mark my words, y'all – like me, with Pasta Club.

Scientists have discovered that ADHDers have differences in brain activity and development from our neurotypical mates. We have impaired 'executive functioning', the brain-boss of organisation, activation, focus and direction. It's also in charge of emotional regulation, arousal activation, problem solving and working memory, and tunes your self-talk radio in or out. Why? Because ADHDers have lower levels of the neurotransmitters called norepinephrine – a building block for dopamine.

Dopamine is what gives us motivation, pleasure and reward. It's generated by healthy sources like sunlight, exercise, sleep, sex, love, food, probiotics, meditation and the ocean, and also from less helpful ones, like sugar, drugs, alcohol, cigarettes, gambling, social media and risky behaviours. Dopamine is a reward-pleasure chemical. This is magnified in ADHDers – if we like what we're doing and feel rewarded by it, then we have both an untapped amount of energy with which to produce it, as well as focus to expand it further.

I have said forever that I operate solely on two speeds: tornado or potato. I am either a million miles a minute as I use interest and pleasure to fuel me, or I am blobbed on the couch, unable to move. Thanks to many trials and tribulations, I've realised my tornado switch is activated by jumping in an hour before a Pasta Club to cook for 60 people at an engagement party because the chef cancelled and there is no kitchenhand. Also, flying across two states to cook at four Pasta Clubs in 72 hours. And working eight days a week to keep the momentum going. The extra energy, hours, focus and attention Pasta Mama needs comes from someplace else, and I think this is the distinguishing factor between those who use their ADHD to their advantage and those who don't.

Without a shadow of a doubt, I know that part of my soul's purpose is to share the genius power that is ADHD. There is nothing that has connected me with more people than this, which frankly is kinda funny, given that for the first 29 years of my life it was what made me feel so distant from everyone else. Wandering around with undiagnosed ADHD is real headknock, but once I discovered that this li'l beastie was my secret gift, the world turned in my favour. Yes, I still struggle with the difficult sides that come with having it, but in the end, I've learned to make the most of all my parts, potato *and* tornado.

CURATED CHAOS

I am potentially Australia's most chaotic and disorganised business owner who nonetheless pulls it from the sky and all together . . . *every single time.* My special sauce seems to reside in the moment of pressure and that tornado switch I just mentioned. Yet, while I'm excelling in delivering creative experiences, my personal world explodes in the background. You'll see me attending fancy marketing events and paid travel trips, but what you don't see is the 23 kilograms of unwashed laundry on my bed, the $7,000 unpaid parking fines built up over the past eight years and a long list of irritated friends who have not heard from me in four months, but watched my glitter-filled life unfold for a heap of strangers on Instagram.

It might look glamorous and successful from the outside, but P Mami has emerged from Plant and Pasta Mama with extreme difficulty, no thanks to my chemical makeup. What it takes to run the admin side of a business happens to be the very kryptonite of an ADHDer, but by some magic juju given to me by the kook gods, I live to tell the tale. It's not ideal, according to the 'Very Serious Business Rules' book, but for this hyperactive, disorganised, flighty, forgetful and overwhelmed gal, building two cult brands with my unique neurodiverse brain was the *only* way it was going to be done.

Let me take you behind the scenes for a moment. Here are a few examples of what's playing out in the three main areas of my life on any given day:

Personal

- I forget to pay bills on time or rack up wild extra charges because of late payments.
- I have time anxiety. I cannot properly predict how long something will take so there is *never enough time* to do anything! Everything feels rushed, important, stressful or on fire.
- I own 15 sets of everything because I lose the other 14 . . . in the house. There are seven of the same hammers in my toolbox and I own 87 hidden hair brushes.
- I am constantly broken, bruised or scratched. (Funny story: I was in *That's Life* magazine when I was 15 for being Australia's most accident-prone teenager.)
- I rarely have a plan for *anything*. I have no idea what is happening in the next hour let alone the next week, month or year.

Relationships

- If you want to be friends with me then you'll need to let go of any communication expectations. I may text you back in five seconds, five months or five years. This does not reflect how much I love you, it's about how many conversations and communications I handle daily and my inability to literally remember who I have spoken to, about what. Sometimes I will read your text and think I have responded when I haven't. It's not personal, it just is.
- You will tell me things and I will absolutely forget them – not all of them, but some of them. Sometimes important things too, which will hurt your feelings. It's not on purpose, I just need to hear things when I am not distracted and am listening in the right environment.
- It's likely I'll be blunt and not sugar-coat things for you. This is typical ADHD and frankly, I appreciate directness. Don't take offence as you'll always know where you stand with me, and if you make the effort to understand my communication style, we will really cut through time.

Work

- If the task is boring, I become as useless as *minus* five people. On the other hand, if it's interesting, I become 10 people in one. Ask me to fold underwear and I'll run the other way, but ask me to cook for 60 people in 10 minutes and I'll grab an apron and run forth.
- Nothing will be done until the day before on any project . . . true fact. My disorganisation levels are unparalleled and have not improved despite my 17,839 attempts at solving them.
- I am a *terrible* emailer – in that I rarely respond to them. However, of the few I do manage to get back to, clients comment on my fun and thoughtful replies.
- I have at least 49 projects on the go at any one time. Working on a single project at one time is what nightmares are made of for me.

YOUR PERSONAL TREASURE HUNT

Now, that was a great little insight into my life, wasn't it? And it just so happens that a lot (but not necessarily all) of it stems from my ADHD. You, YOU, though, will have your own little gifts, quirks and nuances. Own them! Celebrate them! Make them your special powers.

If you are confused about what you are good at or feel that Santa never dropped you a set of personal gifts, let me help you with some gentle cues. Grab a piece of paper and answer the following questions in thoughtful time. Hint: normally your first answer is the one closest to your truth.

Here is a message for EVERYONE: No matter what challenges you face, whether physical, chemical, material or emotional, the sooner you come to accept the shit you cannot change, the better.

- What aspects of your personality or actions do people compliment you on or say are your strengths?
- What activity, action or experience causes the most positive excitement in your life?
- If you had unlimited resources and unlimited time, what would you do with them?
- As a child, what did you enjoy doing most?
- What feels easy to do, yet you love the challenge of wanting to do it better?

Once you have mined these gems for answers, you'll be able to connect some dots and begin your personal treasure hunt. Then use what you find to build a life that perfectly plays to your strengths and minimises your so-called weaknesses. This is how you locate your power, people.

Here is a message for EVERYONE: No matter what challenges you face, whether physical, chemical, material or emotional, the sooner you come to accept the shit you cannot change, the better. You can spend all your energy fighting something that is never going to budge, or you can put that energy into addressing the things you can. The key here is to *do more of what you're good at* while outsourcing the other stuff to people who do it better. Also, find ways to turn your supposed 'weaknesses' to *strengths*. It's all about how you look at your gifts and use them.

Your greatest challenge can also be your greatest power – it's up to you to point it in the right direction using the right perspective.

Rather than calling ADHD a disorder I prefer to call it a gift, because that's how I see it – how I've *chosen* to see it. Getting here wasn't easy. The first three decades of my life were well and truly fucked thanks to this bucking bronco and, even with a diagnosis, it still sends my days up and down. I am sure it will FOREVER. However, after attempting 37,580 ways to banish it from my being, I finally had to accept that it wasn't going anywhere. ADHD has helped create my success. It is the workhorse alongside the intention of my soul and the guidance of the Universe, the three of us working together. ADHD is what generates my truly unique ideas, where the energy to power through multiple large-scale projects comes from and why I take so many risks. If I had to be born again and was asked whether I'd leave my ADHD at the door or take it with me, I would take it with me 88 times over and then some. To think differently and move with unstoppable energy is my blessing.

Once you begin to work with your unique challenges, ask for the support you need, and locate your 'inner genius' within your gifts, you will unequivocally secure the saddle on your own personal wildebeest. Your greatest challenge can also be your greatest power – it's up to you to point it in the right direction using the right perspective.

AUTHENTIC POWER

Every so often I will hear something so powerful explained in my language (layperson's terms) that it just knocks me to the floor in delight. When I read Gary Zukav's book *Authentic Power*, it stopped me dead in my tracks. Zukav explains authentic power as when the personality is in perfect alignment with the soul – you cannot see where one ends and the other begins.

I have no doubt you have met people operating with this power. They stand out in a room and sometimes you can feel them before you see them, but their essence isn't ego or bravado – while assured and powerful, they don't act 'above' you. You believe their words, movements, facial expressions and 'vibe', as their uniqueness comes from a place of self-honesty and commitment to being real.

When we share our authentic selves, including the struggles, we bridge the chasm that separates us from the human experience. Most of us have spent so much time aiming to be perfect we have forgotten how to be authentic. These days it feels like everyone is trapped in a perfection cycle, too scared to share anything for fear of judgement or shame. I was like that too, once, but these days I like to think of myself as a perfectionist control freak in active recovery.

I think developing my authentic self is what's given me my true power. I was recently in a pickle and when I reached out for help, BAM! a long list of stunning helpers came running. A friend asked me how I'm able to do this – what personality trait or *something* do I possess that means I can 'click my fingers' and *multiple* people who are *perfectly aligned* to help show up at random to help solve the problem?

My first response was 'karma' – I quietly go about doing nice things for others so I reckon I might have some good juice tokens saved up or something. But my friend wouldn't accept that. 'No,' she said. 'My husband draws in the same kind of support, but he doesn't go around buying coffee for the random stranger behind him in the line. Try again.'

What you see is what you get, is what's driving my success.

I kept thinking on it . . . What *is* it that makes people show up for me in droves and how have I cultivated this overwhelmingly supportive community of strangers? Beats-fucking-me, honestly. So, I rang around and asked my mates. 'Yo! Why do people love P Mami? What quality attracts people?'

Well, blow me away, the responses were all quite similar and pretty much boiled down to these four things: 1. authentic, 2. blunt-honest, 3. hardworking, and 4. completely unique. (Great exercise, by the way, if you're trying to get to the bottom of that special juju that makes you or your business sing. I highly encourage you to ask the people that know you). As we dove deeper into 'authenticity', it became clear that my success is acutely aligned with how people see me: first, with seeing what I have created in P Mami; and then, when they meet me, realising that the two match up. *What you see is what you get*. People trust me with their time and money because they see truth, vulnerability and honesty.

I am messy, chaotic, colourful and fun and I don't try to hide it.

I am messy, chaotic, colourful and fun and I don't try to hide it. I will happily tell guests at Pasta Club that I cannot cut an onion and have no idea about any wine on the face of the earth other than to mix a $9.99 sack of goon with Golden Circle Passion Punch (especially good when pegged to the clothesline – yo, I see you, my Aussie mates). I don't pretend to be a Michelin-starred chef or know anything about lobster; I make vegetarian home recipes with no measurements other than intuition and a basic understanding of flavours and seasonal food . . . that's literally it. My naivety in the food industry and my disinterest in conforming to the standard expectation of a chef is a factor in my likeability – no bullshit here, just P Mami in the kitchen.

I have not always been authentic. When I was younger, I squished and squeezed my personality to fit into *countless* groups. Ultimately, that made me feel worse. So now I do it differently. These days I don't apologise for who I am and will immediately remove myself from anyone or any group that asks me to change. Period. Getting to this point has not been easy, but hey, we got here. Now my authenticity is what can earn me $10,000 for an appearance (to just *be me)*, what makes me feel whole, and most importantly, what has built my magnificent community of strangers and genuine legends that turn up in all corners of the journey at the right time. To get here, I had to shut down everyone's expectations of me and in the end say, 'Fuck it. I choose me. Always and only.'

THE BUSINESS OF AUTHENTICITY

I have always believed that harnessing your authentic self is one of the most important treks you can take in life, but even more so in business. As both customer and seller, I have witnessed that people invest in what *feels* authentic over a faked appearance of it. We will always prefer engaging with someone who's operating for their soul's purpose – their 'sweet spot'.

One businesswoman who bowled me over with her authenticity when we met is author and entrepreneur Zoë Foster Blake. Before arriving at her house for a plant consultation, I had formed an idea that her 'energy' would be smart and funny. And I was right. But what I didn't expect was to be overwhelmed by how much *more* she was. Zoë was bright, witty, intelligent, charming and matter of fact: the *exact* personality traits of her incredibly successful skincare brand, Go-To.

Attempting to see where *she* ends and *the brand* begins is impossible. This shows an alignment of energy, purpose and personality – authentic power. When I met Zoë, it became very clear to me that a large part of her success is due to people feeling the authentic connection between the founder and the product, with her relatability factor being key to their investment in the product. Whether consciously or unconsciously, people invest in products and in businesses that lead with two things: quality and authenticity. Use your authenticity to grab the customer and your quality to maintain them.

I really believe, to the depths of my soul, that authenticity is key to creating a successful business and life practice. Whether you can recognise it or not, people can *feel* and *sniff* inauthenticity from a mile away and their subconscious mind will always steer them away from this for protection.

Whether consciously or unconsciously, people invest in products and in businesses that lead with two things: quality and authenticity. Use your authenticity to grab the customer and your quality to maintain them.

WHAT AUTHENTIC PEOPLE HAVE IN COMMON

CONSISTENCY WITH IDENTITY

Whether five years or five weeks ago, they are always the same person.

POSITIVELY EMBRACE THEIR FLAWS

They are aware of their weaknesses, switching them to strengths or delegating things they're not good at.

THOU SHALT NOT BE LIKE ANYONE ELSE

Their unique essence is specific to what they bring to the world.

HONESTY FOREVER

They value transparency and vulnerability and are honest about their struggles.

KNOW THEIR GENIUS

They know their zone of genius and operate mostly in this.

DON'T COMPROMISE WHO THEY ARE FOR ANYONE

They show up fully, proudly and uncompromisingly as themselves.

LISTEN TO THEIR INNER VOICE

They know that to silence what is screaming within is a fool's errand. They listen earlier, not later.

ALWAYS GIVE BACK

They are aware of the give-and-take cycle and welcome others to join the ride.

CIAO! IT'S YOUR AUTHENTIC SELF CALLING

Unfortunately for all of us, authentic power doesn't easily land on our doorstep. While it's inside us and something we can locate at any time, when you've been trained or guided to act and behave in a certain way for so long, it becomes hard to separate what you truly want over what others expect from you.

You are no doubt going to meet resistance when you decide to stop pretending and embrace who you are. This is a test – will you prioritise your own needs over someone else's opinion of you? People feel uncomfortable when you change, but would you rather be stuck for the rest of your life because you are avoiding a few hard conversations? Personally, I don't think it's worth it. On the flipside, choosing to be authentic from now on will:

- Attract the best-suited people into your life, the ones who vibrate on your level.
- Unlock magnificent opportunities that will help you grow in the right direction.
- Fast-track progress in identifying your soul's purpose as you move forward.

You must actively move toward finding the thing that is meant for you and be prepared to make changes if what you're currently doing is not working for you. Remember: nothing shifts unless something changes.

Maybe you're thinking that all this self-work seems like a lot – can't I just continue for the next 50 years doing what I am doing? It might be a bit easier. Why is finding your soul's purpose *that important*?

Well, it's for world peace. Kidding! Not really, because it is. When more people are vibrating at their best, it lifts the whole world's experience. Just imagine if everyone felt a level of fulfilment in their day-to-day and comfortable to be themselves? It sounds pretty darn nice to me. I've seen the impact of surrounding yourself with others orbiting in their soul's

When you surround yourself with robots you become a robot, when you surround yourself with kooks you become a kook. So, when you find people who feel authentic, STICK AROUND. It'll rub off soon enough.

purpose. It inspires you to fine-tune your own authenticity radar. When you surround yourself with robots you become a robot, when you surround yourself with kooks you become a kook. So, when you find people who feel authentic, STICK AROUND. It'll rub off soon enough.

We all have a genius quality in us, something that makes us sparkle so much it bursts out of our skin and onto others, creating goodness in the world. The best thing you can do for yourself, your family, your friends and literally *everyone* that walks past you on the street is to try to be the best you can with what you've got. The more you gain, the more you know, and when you know better, you do better.

Life is a really long time and the sooner you start making the majority of your choices with the most honest part of yourself, the easier your days will be. I can promise you that. It has taken all my strength to throw myself into the endless storms of my personal, business and authentic journeys, but weathering them has landed me where I am now. So, there are no regrets – I would do it all 10 times over, even knowing the terrible times ahead.

Inevitably, times will get hard. You can face things at a later date and have less time to enjoy the fruits of your labours, or you can run straight toward what might feel difficult to face right now but is guaranteed to free you from the cage. Follow your internal stirrings, the voices that whisper and nudge you toward an aligned self. They help us know we are heading toward the right self. A satisfied and pleasure-filled self.

We all have a genius quality in us, something that makes us sparkle so much it bursts out of our skin and onto others, creating goodness in the world.

PRINCIPLE 6

Power

Fine-tune your authenticity radar so you can rotate in orbits that charge your power.

Your greatest weakness could also be your greatest strength. Point yourself in the right direction with the right perspective and become your most powerful self.

The sooner you make decisions with the most honest part of yourself, the easier your days will be. Nothing shifts until something changes, so change whatever drains your power.

Ask yourself

What parts of your life activate your tornado switch?

When are you most yourself and find life easiest? When are you most exhausted and depleted?

Name one 'hard part' of being yourself that has an advantage.

On a scale of 1 to 100, how much of your true self shows up in the world? Are you okay with this number?

Name 8 people in your life you are close to and rate their authenticity. Does that affect your ability to be real with them?

chapter seven

PURPOSE

YOUR GREATEST GIFT IS SERVICE

It is your job to work out why you were put on this earth – the purpose of your adventure as you. When you locate what lights you up, it's your job to pay it forward. One of those things for me is consuming donut peaches in summer on the Italian island of Ischia. Another is to share tomato-growing tips, good books, beautiful beaches and interesting concepts. Purpose helps create direction, goals and intentions that offer a life of continuous growth. Ninety years is a long time to spend doing 'okay' – even 10 years feels too much. Your purpose might be to grow the best potatoes in Victoria or maybe to volunteer on weekends at a homeless shelter. It doesn't have to be how you make a living – just whatever you contribute to making the world a better place.

A MEETING WITH THE UNIVERSE

It's 3 pm and I find myself reclining in a soft-yellow bath at my friend's house in Daylesford, reading *The Universe Has Your Back* by Gabrielle Bernstein. At times like this, when Plant Mama is hectic to the extreme, bathing is NOT common behaviour. I can *literally* hear two voices in my head: one reading and the other screaming, 'YOU DIDN'T RESPOND TO THAT EMAIL, DIPSHIT!' Nonetheless, I stay – Gabby's explaining how to make an SOS call to the Universe in times when shiteth-has-hiteth-the-faneth. I have a feeling it might come in handy.

The trick, Gabrielle says, if you find yourself in a world-stopping moment and need help, is to make a mental call to the Universe. First, ask *really clearly* for what you need. Be precise. And do so from a place of *knowing deeply* that the Universe *does* exist, that it *will* help you and the likelihood of help is 100 per cent. Ask and believe and know that no matter what happens, the Universe is always working with you, not against you.

This thought calms my racing mind, but there's still a shit-ton of things I need to get done. I exit the bath chamber in deep thought, taking Gabby's lesson with me.

Fast forward to 4 pm Friday in Melbourne. Folks are either scurrying to Friday-arvo work drinks or already there. My hire van is sitting in a clearway in front of my Plant Mama studio in Collingwood, hazard lights blinking. I am hauling a bunch of giant plants to the car, then gently folding their fronds in under its roof. My first plant drop-off is in Carlton, to my friend Sarah's hair salon. Because I only plan on stopping for a second, I casually drive the van into the laneway next to the salon and although it's blocking the exit to the employee car park, turn the engine off. It's now 4:45 pm.

I jump out of the driver's side and race around to the back of the van, ripping open the rear doors. At the same moment, my keys spin from my hand in a perfect arc high into the air and then, in slow motion, drop ever so cleanly through the welded grate that's covering a 2-metre open drain. Unable to believe my bad luck, I inch over to the grate . . . there in the bottom right corner shine my blue and grey Volkswagen keys.

"FFFFUUUUUUUUUCCCCCCCCCCCCCCK!"

Sarah's salon manager comes running out. 'It will be okay,' he assures me. 'We'll be able to get them out.' As we leap into action, getting nowhere fast, I look up and see that employees from the surrounding buildings are starting to pile into their cars, looking for their weekend escape hatch, only to see a giant blue van stuck in the car park exit. We try putting the car in neutral and rolling it, but it *will not budge*. Every 10 seconds another frustrated driver comes up to ask when we are getting out of there. My head sprouts 15 grey hairs.

More roadblocks appear at every solution. The grate is welded onto the ground so we can't remove it. It's now 5 pm on a Friday – no council guy is coming out. Likewise, the multiple calls I make to the car-rental company ring out unanswered. A builder working onsite next door tries a million different tools, including wrapping heavy-duty double-sided tape onto a steel rod and trying to fish the keys out. We've exhausted all options, and I think I'm about to have a stroke.

The three of us do that thing where you wide-eye stare at one another, hoping someone else has another idea. But, there are no ideas. I am stuck. Like I've never been stuck before.

A lovely tall lady with brown hair who can see how deeply panicked I am hands me some water and suggests I 'take a minute'. Meanwhile, the salon manager chats calmly to the holed-up commuters. Gratefully, I head to an area where no one can see me. I pace back and forward and speak out loud to myself. Gabby's SOS chapter springs to mind. It's the only remaining solution. With nothing to lose, I begin.

'Okay, Universe, this is my SOS call. I need your fucking help RIGHT now. Gabby says I can call on you in times of shitness and I AM HERE! Living and breathing it in hyper-colour. I don't need to tell you that I believe in you – we know this. I have seen the magic happen so I am not going to waste my time convincing you that I know you are there, that you've been there all along. Please, please, PUH-LEEEEEASE can you get me that key in my hands now. I need the key out of the drain. I have tried everything. I have nothing else left to give. I will appreciate this forever if you just give me a chance to solve this. I NEED THAT FARKING KEY IN MY SWEATY HANDS, PLEASE. I BELIEVE YOU WILL HELP ME.'

After three rounds of box breathing (thank you Brené Brown), I emerge from my catatonic state with an empty water glass in hand and a slightly calmer sense of being. The builder has one last tool and calls me over to help guide him. With three of us steering his metal hook to the key, after another five attempts we have to admit: retrieval is impossible.

As I slump to the ground, I hear a voice, kind, curious and raspy. 'Are you right, over there? Lost something down the drain?'

I turn and see an old man. Short, gray hair, a few piercings in his ear, purple vest, no shoes. He has cracked yellow fingernails and arms filled with silver bangles up to his elbows, carrying all his belongings in old and tattered Woolworths bags. He has kind, blue-green eyes and a soul I immediately feel is both sensitive and soothing.

'I've lost my keys down the grate and we've tried everything, but can't get them out,' I wail.

In the slowest of motions, like a movie playing almost backwards, he calmly says, 'Well, what about this?'

He's pointing to a loop on the side of his pants that's holding something silver and shiny. He unclips, pulls up and dangles a long chain in front of us with a magnet attached at the bottom. Much like a crane, he mechanically moves his arm across the drain and efficiently lowers the chain perfectly through the grates. In a mere four-to-five seconds he carefully retrieves the chain and holds it in the air. The van key is swaying on the end. He's smiling proudly. 'Like fishin' in a busy lake!'

We collect our jaws from the floor and leap about, screaming in relief and disbelief. I turn to him with my hand on my heart and offer the deepest, heartfelt thank you. We share a big hug and as we pull apart, I ask if I can do *anything* to help him. I am begging to return the favour.

He rests his yellow fingers and loud bangles on my shoulders, winks his left eye and simply says, 'Just pass it on, love.' He taps me on the side of the cheek and walks away.

People are leaning on their horns. I have no time to absorb what's just happened. I jump in and move the van, releasing the car-park prisoners. I pull over to the side, shaking as they zoom past me to get their Friday-arvo beers. Depleted from overwhelm, I need to retreat from the wildness. I cancel the rest of my plant drop-offs, go home, make a peppermint tea and sit out in my back courtyard for about two hours in complete silence, staring at the sky absorbing the enormity of the situation. This felt like something really big and really special, like I had tangibly seen magic in real life. It needed recognition, space to be remembered forever. While I had believed that the Universe would show up and help, I didn't see it happening in such a dramatic, heart-hitting and obvious way.

Ask and believe.

P.S. Who knew that the Universe was walking around in Carlton wearing a purple vest and a swinging magnet chain?

MISSION PASTA

As every old spiritual folk law states: though you may go searching far and wide, you have had everything you need inside of you all along. From an early age I sponged up the works of all the big spiritual leaders and authors, like Eckhart Tolle and Mitch Albom (I was literally reciting his book *Tuesdays with Morrie* at age fourteen). It meant I got an early shot at beginning the cycle toward my purpose, which is created solely on the basis of two things: curiosity + trial and error.

Through my early teachers, I learned that the energy surrounding what I was doing would clearly indicate if I was on the right course or not. When I look back at my younger self, I made lots of job changes early on if it didn't feel right or the position didn't serve me well outside of pay ('cause no one gets paid well at uni!). This all meant that I churned through the wrong-purpose cycles first and quickly – as with everything I do. It was almost as if something was guiding me to continue the rinse-and-repeat cycle as I nudged closer to what my gift is . . . certainly not folding women's t-shirts into a *perfect square* at Scotch & Soda in Brisbane.

After those early false starts and redirects, locating my purpose has allowed me to feel that 80 per cent of how I'm spending my time is exactly what I want and should be doing with my life. The other 20 per cent is general confusion about what I am actually doing . . . but I feel as though that's the case for everyone. I'm certainly not stupid enough to profess I know the entirety of my purpose – the journey is the majority of the process, Peter!

It would be equally stupid to pretend that finding your purpose is easy. The only way to access your passion and pleasure is to follow the signs of your curiosity or changes in energy – not always the clearest of signals. Annoyingly, finding your purpose might not come as easily as the other principles I share in this book, but it can have the deepest impact on how confidently you walk the path of life. Sometimes it requires much trial and error, along with a commitment to knowing yourself. It takes effort to get serious and get clear on who you are, to peel back the many layers and levels residing inside of you. But I encourage you to persevere!

Much like passion and pleasure, your purpose does not need to come from your work exclusively. Career counsellors have muddied the waters on this one, too. Some people choose to work at the local store because it's a secure position, close to their homes and pays a regular wage. The *purpose* of their job is to cover their essential needs like food, shelter, water, etc. Another *purpose* may

That's the thing about purpose – if you don't know what it is yet, then your passion will lead you to it, and if you can't find your passion, then follow your curiosity.

be providing free educational support to new mums. Perhaps another, to make cabbage edible, I don't know! The point is, purpose can live in a variety of places and is, like everything else, a personal journey.

I know I have a purpose, at some point in my life, of sharing the elderly's thoughts with the world, but I'm waiting for the right space and time for this calling to happen. See, that's the thing about purpose – if you don't know what it is yet, then your passion will lead you to it, and if you can't find your passion, then follow your curiosity. If you cannot locate your curiosity, then just work on getting to know yourself. Simply noticing your reactions to things will make you aware of your energy shifts, and soon enough, curiosity will be knocking on your door. All you have to do is take *one teeny* step at a time.

I created Pasta Club to give people a unique, energy-filled, special dining experience that celebrates creatives and small businesses. Over a few hours, we bring out between 8 and 12 dishes to share and make merry over, with an intimate group of guests – sometimes friends you've gathered together, sometimes strangers. Over Pasta Club's menuless vegetarian and Epicurean feast, you have to let go and trust me and the chefs to do their job – all you can do is sit back, laugh and chat with those around you. The experience is about sharing, creativity and connection, rather than the skills of the artist in the kitchen. And bonus dollars – no cleaning up after!

I wanted to remind folks how simple experiences are fulfilling and fun. From the beginning, my clear, aligned and positive intention has allowed cause and effect to match the driving energy behind it. People are attracted to Pasta Club's energy force; it has special juice. With this, they invest their time, money and energy into being part of something that feels purposeful. And that feels nice for everyone.

The speed at which Pasta Club has grown comes down to people connecting to why it exists in the first place: to show you through my own creative eyes how simple meals with the *right* table of friends can so effortlessly fill up your pleasure cup. My events help you cultivate, in your own way, the sweetness that comes from sharing a meal with people on your level. Somehow, between the pandemic and the formation of UberEATS and prepared meals, we have forgotten why we were eating in the first place. To connect, to nourish and to share.

Intentional purpose

In his book *The Seat of the Soul*, Gary Zukav says that *intention* is at the heart of creating authentic power, calling it the 'why beneath your why'. In other words, the motivation behind all of your choices. I have a very clear mission for Pasta Club, driven by my purpose, my why *behind* the why. This took a while to nut out – my whole lifetime in fact – so lemme hasten the process for you, if you're keen.

The first thing to consider, I think, before deciding on anything is to check in with how you feel. The energy does not lie. Mark Manson, *New York Times* bestselling author of *The Subtle Art of Not Giving a F*ck* offers a great way to figure this out. Is it a fuck yes, or a fuck no? Do my intentions come from a place of love, or are they driven by fear or pain? At the end of the line, you should always be asking yourself: how can I be more thoughtful around my intentionality? Am I acting in alignment with my personal 'why'?

The ability to recognise and consider your 'why beneath the why' will ultimately allow you to dictate your purpose and your fate. By making space to check in, you can interrupt the moment between impulse and action, then consciously act with good intention. Your ability to harness authentic power is directly linked to your ability to move forward based on decisions made in alignment, love and with the right purpose.

Your ability to harness authentic power is directly linked to your ability to move forward based on decisions made in alignment, love and with the right purpose.

ALWAYS HELP A STRANGER – PHILOXENIA AND PHILOTIMO

Each time I visit Greece, the kindness I receive from complete strangers across all generations, socio-economic statuses and genders blows my mind. It was severely tested during my medical nightmare in Samos and the response was an overwhelmingly kind-hearted energy outpouring from every person I met. When I posted my clumsy explanation on Instagram, the responses were equally intoxicating and intriguing:

'*Philoxenia*! You are experiencing what they are most proud of.'

'Kindness & an open home to every traveller.'

'Look up the story of Zeus and Hermes!'

Philoxenia? Activate ADHD hyperfocus Google beast mode, where I deep-dive into a concept or new piece of information, dedicating hours of time and one-track focus into skimming endless websites and articles to ensure I understand every inch. The depth of the rabbit hole is directly related to body position: casually lying on the beach means mild digging, staying indoors on couch/bed means drilling to the earth's core. With *philoxenia* I was fully bed-zoned, digging deep. What a joy to have discovered this!

While the internet offers several different pronunciations that sound like different words altogether, my attempt to convey to you how it sounds is: fill-o-zen-ee-ah. Definitions are slightly clearer: 'love of foreign', 'eagerness to show hospitality' and 'friend to traveller'.

How Zeus rolls

Philoxenia is commonly found among the tales of our fave Greek gods. As well as being head honcho, Zeus was also Patron of Hospitality and Guests, responsible for protecting strangers and travellers. The story goes that he wanted to test his countrymen and their hosting abilities – think of this as Airbnb doing due diligence on hosts, but with 700 BCE vibes.

Zeus disguises himself and his son Hermes and they hit the pavement, whacking on doors to see who will open their homes to offer help. But, as each door remains closed in the face of their knocking, Zeus becomes enraged, ashamed that his community so evidently lacks the core ethos of his existence. About to give up, Zeus gives one last knock on the door of a shambolic shack on the brink of collapse. The door is answered by an elderly couple, Baucis and Philemon, who immediately welcome the strangers with open arms. They have little money and nothing to offer but a meal, wine and a safe place for Zeus and Hermes to lay their heads. Over dinner, Zeus is so overwhelmed by their kindness he begins magically refilling the wine jug each time they fill their glasses, ultimately giving the game away.

Once his identity is discovered he grants the couple their ultimate wish of dying peacefully together – BLESS UP! Then he creates a storm that washes away the homes of the people that had shut their doors to him. Thereafter, it became law to 'always help a stranger' because you never know who is in the room, and because good fortune will rain upon you in exchange for offering hospitality to a traveller.

While protection from the anger of the God of Hospo would be great, the loving behaviour from the Greek people is driven by more than the prospect of good fortune. It's become part of their DNA. Part of their purpose.

In the depths of *philoxenia* research, I discovered another closely linked word: *philotimo*. This pertains to honour and pride in oneself, one's family and one's community while always doing the right thing, honouring dignity and being warm and open to others.

Philoxenia and *philotimo* were presented to me in many ways during my time on the island of Samos – one of the most challenging weeks of my life. As my healing from my appendectomy began, the kindness warriors showed up when I was at my lowest point.

Blessed *yiayias* – my hospital saviours

After surgery I was wheeled into a room of five *yiayias* (Greek for grandmas). And truly, there was no other name for them – the way these roommate angels treated me, that's precisely what they were. I noticed straight away that each had a family member who would sleep in a plastic chair next to them . . . *every . . . single . . . night.* It was quite overwhelming to watch a ninety-year-old husband sleep upright all night, then spend all the next day tending to his wife, cleaning her bedsores and feeding her soup. Day in, day out, without rest.

Where were the nurses, you ask? Overworked, underpaid and understaffed. Aside from pain management (barely there either), patients were on their own. Obtaining water and having a shower? On our own. Accessing basic needs like sanitary products, toiletries and water? On our own. I knew no one on the island, had none of my possessions and was left in the dark regarding post-surgery and an exit plan. I spent every night not sleeping because of my snoring neighbour and most days crying in between naps forced on me by extreme emotional exhaustion. Thank god I had my *yiayias*.

When one of them saw me walking around with a bedsheet as a dress, she hobbled over and gave me her black summer nightie with pink and white flowers on it. Nodding, she handed it to me, making sure I took it. Then, after hearing me crying on the phone to my mum after not showering for four days, the *yiayia* in the bed next to her got her English-speaking daughter to brush my hair into braids. One of their sons helped me translate my hospital report to English, and a husband of another fetched me water and his favourite oregano chips. We could not share much in words, but there was an unspoken love shared between me and these roommates of mine, the women of Samos. Somehow, they wanted to make sure I knew I was never actually *all alone.* The gratitude I feel for these teeny moments of human kindness still make me gush tears if I think about them for too long.

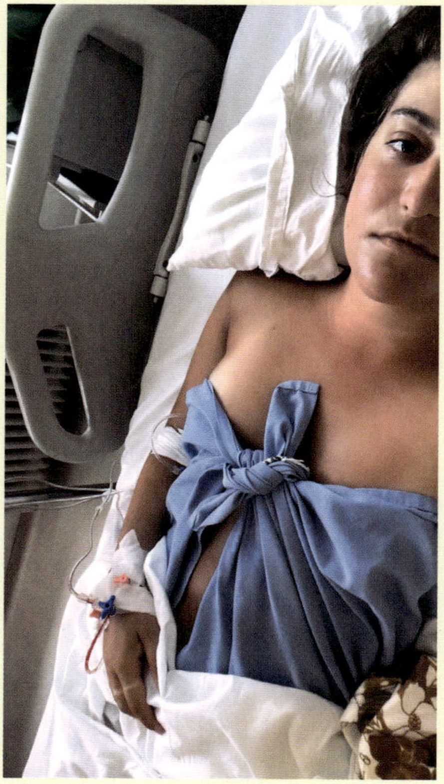

Liz the lawyer – an angel in disguise

On the second day in hospital my phone was dying and the stress just kept mounting. I had no personal possessions with me as all my luggage and belongings were still in the Airbnb on Ikaria. I couldn't speak Greek. I had no idea of my plan for recovery or when I was supposed to be getting out of there. All I knew was that my phone had 10 per cent charge and I needed help – someone to bring me underwear, a toothbrush and toiletries. I couldn't keep wearing oversized sanitary nappies as my period saviours, I just couldn't. Not for another moment.

I thought it was worth a last-ditch attempt to go on Instagram and ask for help. As you know by now, I have built a really strong community there that shows up in times of need. I thought there might just be *one* person out there who follows me that was from Samos or knew someone who was, and since I had no one else to ask, it was time to post: a Google maps screenshot of the island tagged, *SOS! Anyone in Samos??*

Instantly, I had a few responses, but as always, one stood out. This time from Liz, thirty-something, lawyer, Melbourne/Samos. 'I am on Samos!' she wrote. 'How can I help?'

Liz and her family were onto it, *straight away*. Within hours, my new-found stranger-become-friend had instantly graduated to sisterhood level. She burst through my hospital door like an angel sent from above with an Australian accent and the warmest smile I have ever witnessed. In a bag she carried undies, face sprays, chargers and everything I needed, plus more. As to be expected, I began crying again. Liz and her family showed up all week for me, collecting my hand luggage from other islands and arriving to check me out of hospital with all the info I needed. That family really went above and beyond for me, something that will be engraved on my heart forever. They well and truly saved the day by servicing my basic needs when I was completely broken.

After five days too long in hospital I was eventually released – but only to rest at a local hotel until I was approved to fly. As I paid my bill at the hospital admin office, my courage and strength returned. In no uncertain terms I communicated the full terror of my experience to the hospital administrator, outlining how poorly I was treated by certain staff. As I was leaving, the female anaesthetist gave me her business card and told me to text or call her if I had any problems. While normally a card tosser, my intuition told me to keep this one, so I tucked it safely away.

Vicki and Eleni – my healing soul sisters

As we drove away from the hospital in Liz's car, I was probably at my most raw ever. We arrived at the hotel and I walked into a gleaming white, airy lobby that had an incredibly beautiful, open energy – the complete opposite of the hospital's. Blame the stunning white marble or blame my emotional state, but I started crying again.

Straight away, Liz jumped into Greek-speak and explained my traumatic and terrible time to the receptionist, Eleni. 'Don't worry,' Eleni said, taking my hand. 'You'll be safe here.'

And she was oh so right. In the peace of that clean, nice room with my own shower, bed and silence, I was transported from hell to heaven. My first meal was an orange juice and a chicken club sandwich and I spent the first three days at the hotel sleeping and staring at the wall, still in shock. I felt like I'd been sucker-punched by the Universe and needed time to absorb it. Not punched in an ugly way, like I'd done something wrong, but in a sit-up-and-take-notice kind of way.

I felt overwhelmed by what I'd just experienced and needed to sit in what had just occurred and what it now meant. Post-surgery I was advised not to lift anything heavy for the next six weeks . . . like my 40 kg suitcase. My dream of spending two months writing this book on a Greek island while sipping iced coffees and slurping Greek yoghurt and honey had just been cancelled. I'd been completely ignored by one group of people (hospital staff), but seen and cared for by others (*yiayias*, Liz, anaesthetist, hotel receptionist) – all of them complete strangers. I needed space – a lot of it – to make sense of it all.

The following day at breakfast, Eleni and her colleague Vicki checked in to see how I was feeling. Each day they went out of their way to look after me, making me my favourite foods and drinks and helping translate all my hospital and insurance forms. Vicki offered to go back to the hospital with me when it came time to remove my stitches, acting as my spiritual/power-sister bodyguard.

Vicki would bring me freshly picked grapes from the hotel vineyards and chocolate snacks to my room, while Eleni organised a friend of hers, George, to drive me around to see the island. While waiting for my lunch to be made each day, I would sit at the bar and eat vanilla ice cream as Eleni smoked at the bar inside and Vicki made me Greek coffee from her own recipe (outstanding!). We would talk about their families, past jobs, secrets of the island – basic gal chat. As each day passed and we exchanged more things about one another, we began building a lovely and genuine connection, which by the end felt like a reunion between old sister-friends. I met Vicki's young son at the pool (as smiley and warm as her) and Eleni showed me her plans to build a seaside oasis that I promised to visit upon my return the following year.

But the thing I loved most about them was, *before* we'd even had the chance to talk and decide if we liked one another, both women had assumed the practices of *philoxenia* and *philotimo*. They saw a woman down and in need of healing, so they showed up with kindness and provided me with the love I needed in a time riddled with heartbreak and disconnection. I believe they were there to balance the story out. To remind me that sisters don't just come running from your home orbit; that help is a collective effort and always on offer, wherever you are in the world.

Anthony – Athenian hero taxi driver

Anthony the Athenian taxi driver was the bookend to my Samos angels. I first met him when I arrived in Athens on my way to visit the Greek islands. During our 30-minute ride to my hotel, he was very chatty, suggesting lists of islands to visit and things to check out. Initially, I remained alert and defensive, as any solo female traveller does when alone in a strange male's presence, especially in the taxi of one. I have seen the movie *Taken*, guys – I know what can happen.

After about 20 minutes my energy radar had done its work – I'd assessed his early-40s kind face and heard about his pre-teen son holidaying with his mum – and I felt assured that Anthony (Tony) was a friendly, harmless and helpful stranger. I left his cab with his phone number and a long list of recommendations, plus the phone number of a friend to reach out to if I hit a particular island.

Flash forward to post surgery. I was getting ready to leave Samos and fly back to Melbourne with a short stopover in Athens. Confined to a wheelchair, I needed help. There were items that needed to be collected from different shops across Athens, things I had planned to do myself when leaving the country: film negatives, camera pieces, tax receipts for refunds and an array of other important things. This task would take a few hours and on the most inconvenient day (a public holiday) during the most inconvenient time of the day.

When I reached out to Tony and explained my situation and my offer to pay him, he leaped at the opportunity to help and repair any broken feelings toward Greece. After what turned into a several-hour mission, Tony turned up to the airport sweating and clutching all my important documents, which he had folded

and tied together with such care. I finally had everything I needed to fly home. While sitting at the flight gate waiting to board, I texted him a deep thank you.

It's okay, I love to help, he replied. *I am Greek. It's what we do. Pick you up next August.*

Yes, Tony. *It is* what you do, it's what *you all do*. So naturally, so intrinsically, so easily and with no expectation of exchange, simply for the delight in helping someone.

My list of *philoxenia* experiences could go on forever. They are all stories of warmth and help toward me, the foreign traveller. What a goddamn blessing to have an overflowing bucket of kindness stories that has no end. If you are looking to feel the ultimate human experience then head to Greece, where you will find *philoxenia* and *philotimo* out in full force, a thoughtful and connected way of life. But, you need not be on the Aegean shores in order to experience or be an agent of these ways, oh no, no, no! You can be kind to a stranger in your own neighbourhood, and you can also just do a small, nice thing for someone with no strings attached.

Your purpose in life does not need to be meaningful only if you are doing something in full service to help others. No person and their purpose is more important than anyone else's; we value and desire different things. But, if you find yourself in moments where you can help, then you should. Sometimes, we offer a hand back to help, and sometimes we must put a hand forward to receive. You'll never regret doing either of those things.

A WORD ON SUPPORTING CREATIVES

When I was a small fry and just starting out in business, lots of people took a chance on me and helped me out, hiring me with not much experience, but an understanding of what I was trying to achieve. I was working toward my purpose of sharing my creative gifts with the world, but there is no way I could have made it without the support of others. I knew all along that this was gifted to me, this good fortune – of being seen and supported by others – and one day it would be my turn to pay back.

Something my small-business-owner mother taught me is, don't forget that the little fish (small businesses) are just as important as the big fish (big brands) and are often nicer to play with. In other words, don't let big promises dictate who you work with. I know first-hand that the little fish have the capacity to create meaningful experiences and must not be forgotten in favour of grandeur. As a creative person (which everyone is in some way), it's your duty to share opportunities that expand others' prospects. Everyone deserves at least one person to believe in them.

Spaghetti sisters

This little-fish-and-loyalty story is a sweet tale involving a local Collingwood business owner. During the pandemic I launched an idea that had been rolling around for a while, the 'spaghetti cap' – a cute range of hats with 'spaghetti' embroidered on the front panel. Behind my house was a small studio, Winston Embroidery. Over a few months, its lovely owner, Julia, and I worked together to finalise the cap's design.

Each interaction helped build our friendship and small-biz bond. Julia followed me on Instagram and if ever she saw I was sick or in need of something, she offered help without hesitation. One day, I called her to put in an order. When she asked how I was, I burst into tears over my poor attempts at bookkeeping the business's finances. Julia stayed on the phone with me for about 40 minutes, calming me down with her soothing words, then offered to come over and help as 'finances were her thing'. Hopping off that phone call, I felt wrapped in a warm, safe hug.

Over the next few years, various business advisors suggested I leave Julia's business and take my embroidery to China to save an extra $4 per cap. In a not-so-roundabout way I told them to GET ABSOLUTELY FUCKED. I will never do that . . . EVER. Even for free. It just will not happen. Julia supported me when I was down and her loyalty is worth so much more than the few thousand dollars I could save.

My dedication to my small-business alliances will always outweigh monetary benefits. We are a tribe. Support the underdog, notice the little fishes and choose loyalty first to the right people. Part of my purpose includes the deep desire to share this concept about how we can best support each other in our small-biz allyship. Together we can move mountains.

Bloomin' legend

Recently we took Pasta Club interstate, visiting several areas of Australia for the first time. I needed some flowers for an event in Noosa, so I did an Instagram call-out for a florist. As usual, I was flooded with responses and so began the task of sifting through them to find someone who would nail the brief. 'Your Bud' florist had messaged me sounding bright and keen to do the job. She only had about 200 followers, but I liked the photos of her work. Other well-known Sunshine Coast florists also sent proposals. As always, I chose the underdog . . . and how glad I am! The lovely Sarah rocked up to the event with *way more* flowers than I'd paid for. Our quick chat revealed she had travelled from Brunswick – three hours EACH WAY – because she said, 'When Pasta Mama calls, you come running!'

Sarah wanted to work with Pasta Mama, so thought she'd go for it, even though it meant a full day driving. Meeting her was a shooketh-the-heart, tear-worthy moment, as I recognised myself in her. When I began my business, I would have done the same to work with someone I admired. I believe iconic-underdog behaviour will always get you far – connections created off the back of a solid work exchange are a wonderful thang.

THE PRICE OF CREATIVITY

The price of creative thought has been a highly contentious subject since the beginning of my earliest business, Plant Mama. Initially, when quoting and charging for my indoor-plant-design concepts, I tried to find the balance between being realistic about my experience while not undervaluing my creative worth. Unfortunately, I think I undersold myself. What I have learned over the years, working as a creative myself and in partnerships with other artists, is that you should *never underestimate or undervalue* creative contributions as their cost normally reflects *exactly* the effort.

In other words, don't be that arsehole that second-guesses a quote and penny pinches on the creative element because it's difficult for you to quantify (in unit terms) what its 'value' is. Despite the unhelpful notion that creativity is an endless stream of great ideas and easy work, it's NOT. Creativity is a stubborn, sensitive, highly fickle beast that is not easily tamed. Those that 'appear' to pluck something out of the ether 'like magic' can only do so after years and *years* of honing their skills and muchos muchos time and effort put into developing and maintaining their creative juju.

There is nothing more soul destroying to a creative person than hearing someone say, 'I could have done that!' Yeah, Jared, well ya fucking didn't! If that painting was so simple you could *easily have done it yourself*, then why haven't you? I don't see a gallery full of your work, mate. To paraphrase an idea from Brené Brown – I'm not interested in your feedback unless you are in the ring too, getting your arse whipped.

The successful creative people I know who are excelling in their careers are doing so because they do not budge on the value of their art for anyone. I recommend this approach if you're a creative. This sets the expectation that you know your worth, and also demands respect from those looking at your art. Others will value you the way you value yourself. So set the price you deserve. I mean heck, in 1961, artist Piero Manzoni made thousands from selling his literal shit, titling the production 'Artist's Shit' – and it's now worth hundreds of thousands of dollars!

You are the only one who knows what it took to get here – the hours you put in and the knowledge gained from all the fuckups along the way of practising your gift to the point of insanity. If your purpose is to create art for selling and it's meant to be a fully functioning business with its own pressures and costs, then life will direct you toward that reality. Likewise, if painting is a quiet hobby

you would rather not share with anyone but your four walls and fur baby. The choice is yours.

Whatever you put out, the Universe will send back your way, tenfold. So be clear with your intentions. Stay focused and travel in support of your purpose and the Universe *will* have your back.

Creativity is a stubborn, sensitive, highly fickle beast that is not easily tamed. Those that 'appear' to pluck something out of the ether 'like magic' can only do so after years and *years* of honing their skills and muchos muchos time and effort put into developing and maintaining their creative juju.

PRINCIPLE 7
Purpose

Your purpose plays at your heart strings. If you're not sure what it is, just follow your curiosity. When you find it, it will feel like closing a circle.

Your deeper intention – your why behind your why – will determine the result.

It's your job to locate and share your unique gifts with the world. What energy imprint will you leave behind and will it reflect your truest self?

Ask yourself

Why do you think you are here?

How active are you in designing your life adventure?

Write down 3 things that bring meaning to your life. Why do you do them? What is your intention behind them?

List some experiences you've had of giving and receiving *philoxenia* and *philotimo* in your own day-to-day life.

How can you pay your gifts forward?

PLACES

chapter eight

THE JOY OF LOOSE TRAVEL

As I have arrived and departed from many places in the Mediterranean and my homeland Down Under, each place, regardless of the hours or the weeks spent there, has left its imprint. Whether as inspiration in my creative practices or the memory of fresh-plucked fruit, each visit has contributed to the larger meaning I seek. To see how life unfolds when you live in another place, what is common between us, what is different, and what I can learn to make my personal environment richer than it was yesterday. As we move about, whether across towns or countries, we can shake up our reality by seeing that the big world out there runs and operates regardless. The planet turns, even when we think it will stop, and learning to find pleasure in travel gifts us the opportunity to experience how others live. By simply standing in a different place, you can open yourself up to multiple ways of being, which, trust me, is the only way to live.

There are wonderful gifts to explore if you open your front door and take a few steps. It's a marvellous, glorious, sublime and delightful world out there.

ROMAN SPIRIT MAN

While lessons often come from unexpected people and places, I reckon most of us would agree that travelling is guaranteed to deliver them in spades – I mean, that's part of the point, no? Still, there are ways and there are ways. I'm learning to listen before I get beat.

It's 2011 and my first time in Rome. I've arrived on a 5 am flight and, unable to check in to my accommodation, decide to walk the streets – in awe, of course! Around mid-morning I pop into a little espresso bar and order a 'takeaway' coffee. The barista looks at me like I have three heads. Still, he grabs a tiny plastic cup, like the ones at the dentist, and begrudgingly hands me my espresso.

I see no problem with this exchange and continue my walk down Via Del Corso. I pass a giant building; outside sits a guy on a small chair. He has a laminated newspaper article beside him, headlined: 'Best Palm Reader in The World'. I continue walking, but seconds later my inner voice screams, 'Go back!'

Trusting my intuition and curiosity, I turn back to the tall man in the fedora hat. He is maybe 60 years old with kind eyes and a cheeky smile. I ask how much for a reading.

'Forty euro,' he says.

'No way!' I reply. 'That's nearly eighty Australian bucks. How do I know you're not scamming me?'

'Okay,' he says. 'You pay half today and if something I predict happens in the next twenty-four hours, you come back and pay me the other half.'

Ya gotta deal, Roman Spirit Man! We sit down.

Truly unprepared for what is about to go down, at the same time I'm truly open to receiving whatever he says. I like this about myself – that I'm able to remain open when there's something I don't know about, or have yet to experience. I believe *this* practice brings me so many wonderful delights – because I'm open to receiving them.

Straight up, Spirit Man asks, 'Why are you in Italy? For holiday or work?'

'Holiday!'

'Okay, so if you are on holiday, what, you don't have five minutes to sit and enjoy your espresso in Rome? What are you off rushing to see exactly?'

BOOM. BOOM. BOOM. Without knowing me at all, he has summed me up in 10 seconds flat. I am the queen of rushing everywhere, never able to stop, sip and take in the serenity. I constantly feel rushed, as if I'm chasing time and the to-do list will never end. As I pick my jaw up from the floor, he opens my palms and spends some minutes studying them. Then he downloads, for 15 minutes, everything he sees either *now* in my persona or predicts for my *future*, including:

You will have a house in Italy and go between the two with your family when you are older.

You won't stay in the state that you are living in, but will go somewhere south in Australia to a major city.

Other people will work for you one day.

You will have one passionate partner that is short term and a long, meaningful relationship with someone else, but that will come later for you than everyone else, maybe in your mid-30s, so just trust.

Teaching will not feed you what you desire, it will tire you within a few years.

Your gifts are in working with nature and with colours – something to do with your hands.

You bring people together and connect them – this is your greatest personal asset.

His parting comment is, 'Jenna, you need to learn to slow down or else it will cost you your life. You have so much going on up there,' he says, waving his hands at my head, 'that if you do not stay present and grounded, something will happen. There's no need to rush, okay? I'll see you tomorrow for the other half.'

This really hits home because I know it is true. My entire life I have been told to *slow down*, but for the first time, I feel as if I've *really* heard it. I immediately call Mum to relay what a wonderful experience I've just had. I tell her I am a changed woman, that I'll be more present and stop rushing and all the rah-rah-rah we like to tell ourselves. Soon after, I make my way to the grocery store, then head toward my accommodation.

As I step off the bus with earphones blasting music in my ears, I walk behind the bus, check the traffic is clear to my right, then step onto the road – completely forgetting that Italians drive on the other side. As I step blindly out into three lanes of oncoming traffic, something makes me look up. I clock the chaos hurtling toward me as the world moves in slo-mo. I drop all my bags on the ground, fully prepared to get hit.

As if by some fucking miracle, the red car racing toward me swerves to a halt, missing me by centimetres, its owner *screaming* while everyone else leans on their horns. Barely able to breathe, I grab my handbag, leave my groceries spilled across the road and stumble to my room. For about 20 minutes I sit on my bed in complete silence, trying to recover from what just happened. I lie down and scroll Facebook for a mindless dopamine hit and Oprah's face fills the screen.

As always, she delivers me a punch-one-two, as if she has just witnessed what's gone down in Roman town and intends to remind me of the lesson. *This needn't have happened*, she basically says. *If you ignore the series of whispers and warning signs the Universe sends you, eventually a brick wall will fall on your head. But you can avoid all that if you just listen.*

First thing next morning, I withdraw €20 from the ATM and hand it over to my Roman Spirit Man.

Now, just in case you cannot read between the lines here, EVERY SINGLE ONE of his predictions has COME TRUE (except the mid-30s meaningful partner, 'cause duh, I'm not there yet). He more than earned his full €40 fee – his predictions have proven priceless. None of which I'd have accessed without going there.

THE GIFT OF FREEDOM

Blame my Aquarian nature or my inability to sit still with my hyperactive ADHD tendencies in tow, but I am *constantly* on the move. Over 32 years on earth I have lived in Toowoomba, Brisbane, Melbourne, Byron Bay, Sydney and even Tuscaloosa, Alabama (USA). I have also explored the world, as travelling is in my top-three most important things in life (the other two being fresh donut peaches and Meryl Streep films). In the last year, I have not had a permanent home by choice, moving around with my dog and important belongings in the back seat of my car. While all my furniture has been locked in storage, I've been gallivanting across Australia, serving Pasta Club with joy and delight.

Yet I'm probably more aware than anyone just how important it is to create a safe space to melt into at the end of a day. As a visual person first and foremost, I rely heavily on aesthetics to dictate my mood. Through nature, plant jungles, feast tables of colour and designing a space from start to finish, I wholeheartedly understand the effect a space has on the person who enters it. From the type of music playing, to the position of the speaker, to where the lighting sits in the room and how far the furniture is from the dance floor, I am passionate about creating the right setting for my over-sensitive senses. And somehow, these spaces became environments that others wanted to experience too, and so here we are – with me gifting my aesthetics wherever I land.

Travelling is in my top-three most important things in life (the other two being fresh donut peaches and Meryl Streep films).

I think many of us don't consider the effect that a space or place can have on us, as if the impact of our environment is somehow irrelevant. Do you relax into a space and open up because it makes you feel comfortable, or just exist on uncomfortable furniture because you're willing to make do? Have you thought about what your mind and body deserve? For me, as with everything, the optimal space has nothing to do with grandeur. I've been in some pretty schmick houses thanks to Pasta Club, and while jaw dropping, they often feel cold, while a mate's one-bed flat above a fish-and-chip shop in Melbourne I rate as the warmest hug-of-a-home I've ever been in.

We have confused fancy furniture, big houses and expensive art with happiness – so much so, that we've forgotten *we* are the ones who choose the space around us. I believe the places you draw inspiration from do not need to be fancy. A park on the other side of town, a beach a few hours away, or even a staycation at a hotel in your home city: every place has something to inspire us or teach us.

It's not necessarily about taking a flight to a fancy destination (Italy and Greece always excepted), but more about finding beauty and inspiration in the most random and isolated places. Getting outside our comfort zone can sometimes feel overwhelming, but there are wonderful gifts to explore if you open your front door and take a few steps. It's a marvellous, glorious, sublime and delightful world out there. So, let me show you how we move around, P Mami style!

THE ART OF LOOSE TRAVEL

Over my years of travel, I have come to realise that travelling overseas and injecting yourself into another culture is a fast way to learn a lot about yourself. Even on meticulously planned trips, disasters still occurred, so I quickly decided that 'loose travel' is how I move best and where the most impactful (83 per cent positive, 17 per cent negative) opportunities lie for me. The best recommendations that lead to the highest amount of pleasure come from the locals. Always.

Too many firm bookings leave no space for spontaneous off-the-beaten-track moments, which are THE BEST PART OF TRAVEL! (Done safely of course!) Leave your schedule open and trust that you will be sent wherever you need to go. The Universe does not stop working with you because you left your place of residence for a few weeks – let it and your intuition do the work as you would in your everyday life, with the added spice of being in a completely fresh environment.

I have travelled alone and with others, with a car and without one, and I have had enough accommodation and flight failures to encourage anyone to immediately burn their passport. When taking overseas trips with others, you learn quick-smart about your companions' adorable habits, idiosyncrasies and inability to order off a menu. Travelling puts you in situations that generate a level of stress not found at home. While you can follow as many precautions as your little perfectionist mind desires, the end result is that bumps will arise, no matter how well you plan. The richest of travellers and the poorest of travellers experience the same travel hiccups – no one is immune to a missed flight, an overseas ATM scam or a hotel that misrepresents itself online.

BUT, HALF THE FUN IS THE ADVENTURE! Trust yourself, follow your intuition, search for Airbnbs and lean into your self-guided travel adventure. Over many years, I've figured out the best approach is to mix things up: revisit some old favourites and step out into some new ones. You try different spots and some take a piece of your heart to become your new 'old favourites', while others you hope to never hear of or see again. It's all part of the fun.

Please use my tips as a portal to dip thy toe into open travel, but also find the courage in yourself to create your own path. Find your personal travel angels along the way and let them guide you to unique experiences. The Lonely Planet guides send every man and his dog to the same pub in England and the same club hotspot or best hotdog for under $5. Avoid them like the plague! Part of the wonder and

delight of travel is putting your trust in the unknown. As long as you have money in the bank, a healthy body and travel insurance, things can't go too far wrong.

Here is a list of things to consider when taking your next trip. Let my mistakes be your wonderful lessons! To give context, I am a lazy traveller who is hyper focused on Italy and Greece which have consumed 90 per cent of my 13 years of travel, therefore my advice pertains to these countries. I'm also the first to caution you that someone else's travel tips must always be taken with a grain of salt. However, I'm confident these goodies can be used when visiting the many countries and places of ze world.

Take my Mediterranean knowings as a broad guide, but be excited to run head first into your own soul-fulfilling experiences that will shake you up with love if you are willing to let go for a little bit. Trust that you'll land exactly where you need to and will receive exactly what you need in that moment. Every place, meal and person has something to teach us on our travels – all you have to do is *open up*.

Bookings

There is no doubt that booking things late will cost you more money and booking things way in advance will have an impact on your flexibility on the trip. It comes down to asking yourself: do I spend more money and go 'unplanned' with the ability to change direction at any time? Or do I save money and map out the exact itinerary of the trip?

I tend to find myself leaning more toward unplanned travel with a few specific elements booked in advance, like unique accommodation I want to try, or necessary flights. Open travel is more stressful, but can lead to the discovery of amazing things, whereas a planned trip might allow you to relax more. Booking your flights and accommodation can be done via a travel agent or, like myself, by googling the best deals online.

It's completely standard practice for me to book my accommodation on the morning I arrive. This anti-plan would send many people into a tizzy, but somehow it continues to deliver me the gems I seek, mainly because I see the power in remaining uninhibited when you travel and what can unfold if you stay relaxed.

Accommodation

Your two main accommodation options in Europe are either hotels or privately owned apartments – B&Bs/Airbnbs, each with pros and cons. I like to mix it up. An apartment has its own kitchen, more space to relax and play your music and generally offers a more 'homely' stay. You may also experience shitty beds, terrible pillows, towels thinner than toilet paper and the potential of hidden cameras. Also, the Sardinian host of your dreams and real-life experiences. Hotels, on the other hand, are great when you need fresh towels, a reliable internet connection and sound sleep. Make sure your hotel is surrounded by plenty of restaurants as most don't have cooking facilities.

My best stays have been mini self-contained cabins, typically sitting on a winery or farm with an attached restaurant that serves breakfast (included) and offers farm-to-table dining at night. You'll find these spread all throughout Italy and Greece, especially in my favourite, Sardinia. Follow this tip + your curiosity.

Food

The most exciting thing about travelling is, no doubt, the food. Shovelling local cuisine into your trap at every opportunity – pure joy! As I love to cook, I enjoy both eating out and cooking at home in a new country. Consuming local products at their freshest and best is a wonderful thing. Italian tomatoes. White wine from local grapes. Fresh-plucked figs. Savouring these delights is nothing short of ecstasy, and they're often found in the local mini mart.

Of course, part of travel's delight is also not having to cook. Sometimes Mario making me spaghetti is a lot nicer than me making me spaghetti. Google reviews help steer the restaurant-choice decision, but mostly I trust my intuition (and the locals) to guide me.

Packing

Have you ever dragged 40kg of luggage along cobblestone streets in Naples for four kilometres during the scorching midday heat because the taxi drivers were on strike? Yeah, well I fucking have and it's officially cooked. I may never recover from that – and the midway lemon granita did absolutely nothing to ease the pain.

What can we learn from this? Two things. Firstly, I don't care how many times you tell yourself this: you *will not* wear those 33 outfits and four pairs of heels you don't even wear in ordinary life. You will recycle three to four key outfits the entire trip and wish you'd packed only carry-on luggage. Learn from past me – pack light and be specific.

Secondly, invest in *good-quality* luggage. This is a golden tip, as the ease with which you wheel your belongings will majorly impact your stress and mood. Anything less than $200 will lose a wheel within two hours of use. Don't be stingy; invest in this. If you purchase something high quality that's right for you, you'll be less likely to need to replace it. Quality stands the test of time – it's a fact.

Cash

Always carry cash! *Always.* I cannot tell you how many times I have been screwed because I was not carrying the local currency. Not every city is on the PayPass or tap & go and while you do not need to carry around $10,000 to be safe, I would suggest always having at least $60 handy.

To drive or not to drive?

Hiring a car in Europe (especially in Italy and Greece) comes down to one main question: how anxious are you on the roads? If the answer is 'medium to high' then sorry, go public transport. If you're a confident driver who can maintain a level head in stressful situations welcome to the best gift of travel: CAR FREEDOM!

Why? TO SEE MORE! Simple as that. While buses and trains exist, they tend to cover a limited area – obvious towns and tourist spots. As I like to visit the quieter towns where no one speaks English and there is only one restaurant, a car is best for me. I've had some of the best meals *in my life* at random-arse towns we drove through after a morning on the beach. Having car keys expands the possibilities of your exploring. Different beaches every day, different grocery shops with different snacks, and the option to control your time and speed with the flexibility to change at any point.

Travel buddies

Oh, WHAT a contentious subject and one of my all-time faves to discuss. Who can you travel with and who can you not? The journey to discover this answer has ruined many friendships and I have an endless supply of evidence from close friends as to how lethally wrong a bad-travel-buddy combo can go.

Luckily, these are not my personal experiences, because I identified during my early travels with friends in my twenties what personalities did and didn't work with me on my travelling journey. As an introvert, and since travel is such a delight and a visual inspiration to me, often during the 'end of day' period when regular folk like to head to dinner, I prefer to sit alone in my apartment and stare at the Mediterranean Sea. Finding someone who won't be offended by such needs is crucial and while I sound like a Negative-Nelly-No-Friends with my solo travel desires, I am lucky to have found the perfect travel buddy in my friend Isabella. We bring out the best in each other, so with three European tours under our belt, we have a promise to continue touring well into our 70s.

A SUMMER LOVE AFFAIR

Every time a European summer approaches and I can make it happen, you will find me in two places only: Greece and Italy. From my first visit in 2001, and every time I've visited since, they whisper to me upon arrival, 'Welcome home, sis.' From the get-go, the people, food and beaches of these lands summoned a special kind of peace in me that allowed me to reset, downshift and recalibrate before returning home to the hustle-bustle work life.

When I thought about a word for each country, it was 'love' for Italy and 'kindness' for Greece. We have a thing, the Greeks, Italians and I. At a festival in Florence when I was 26, I remember looking around and being shocked that I would happily have slept with 89 per cent of the festival goers due to their attractiveness, compared with Australian festivals where my attraction levels peak at 0.34 per cent on the first day and go rapidly downhill after that.

For nine months of the year, I work with a maniacal zeal in exchange for three months of Greek and Italian sun-time – my idea of a life worth living, since the only way I can relax is to physically remove myself from my business by switching time zones. Since everyone is asleep on the other side of the world, I'm forced to take a vacay. My hyperactive-perfectionist-control-freak-workaholic-overthinking-mind-masking-my-struggles self takes a backseat and I enjoy my six favourite things in one fantastic experience: reading a book on a beach in the sun, enjoying a bag of cold fresh fruit, sparkling water and a locally rolled spliff from my Airbnb host.

Each time I return to the Mediterranean way of life I am revitalised. Somehow, with the same number of hours, its people enjoy an existence that puts connection, community, food and living life at its heart. Of course, the slower way comes with its own problems – younger generations aren't keen to stay among such quiet regions that have experienced their own socio-economic crisis and pandemic struggles. I can imagine being a 16-year-old stuck in the Sardinian hills with no internet would really suck. A faster-paced eye might suggest these areas should modernise and create efficiencies, but most Greek and Italians believe: if it ain't broke, don't fix it. Generally, this way of life works for them and they are in no hurry to adjust. You come to us, you live like us.

Every trip I make to these miracles on earth builds my belief that it's possible to find the sweet spot between work and play – an existence where the enjoyment of living equals the work effort, and neither dominates. This lifestyle starts with a belief in abundance – the life of plenty – and the knowledge that more good stuff is just around the corner: a fresh bowl of gelato and afternoons by the ocean.

This lifestyle starts with a belief in abundance – the life of plenty – and the knowledge that more good stuff is just around the corner.

Travelling to these countries will gift you:

- *An understanding* of how food is a nourishing and pleasurable experience. Not in a dramatic over-the-top way, but rather with simple flavours and minimal ingredients, eaten seasonally. You haven't tried the perfect tomato until you've eaten one fresh from a Tuscan vine. Bet my life savings on it.
- *An appreciation* for the older members of the community – our wisest compadres. Both Greece and Italy have an unwavering respect and care for the elderly. It's not a family's job to care for their elders, but rather the entire community's.
- *A clear view* of how place, community, food and connection are intrinsically linked. People eat together – sharing food and plates, swapping produce, cooking for each other, leaving bags of zucchini tied to your front door. Through food, they love.
- *A life less digital* and how *wonderful and easy* life remains without its interference. Reading a book on the beach is so much nicer when you cannot stream Netflix on your phone or scroll TikTok.
- *An appreciation* of your beach body – regardless of its shape or size. The love, adoration and acceptance of everybody on the beach is powerful. Why does wearing one particular bikini in Australia make me feel *so uncomfortable and insecure* yet the same bikini worn on the Isle of Capri asserts a Beyoncé-circa-2007 vibe? Because, regardless of what advertisers class as 'beach ready', *every* human body type is on the sand in Italy and Greece. No one denies themselves the enjoyment of swimming in the ocean. Nothing to see here!
- *A culture and cohort* who deliver an abundance of warmth, hospitality, openness and kindness. Of course, there are jerks everywhere, in Greece and Italy too, but 99 per cent of the population is deeply wonderful and will foster a meaningful connection with you, if you are open to it.

So, do it! Book your ticket and make your way toward one of the most fulfilling life adventures available. The Greeks and Italians are a proud and stoic lot – with varying histories, subcultures, political intentions, food interests and arts distinguishing each region. While awash with their own unique features, I can confirm that no matter where you place your feet here, you are guaranteed to leave more inspired than you were before you arrived. You will learn the ultimate *dolce vita*. The sweet life, waiting just for you. *Molto bene* – very good.

ITALY – THE LAND OF LOVE

I love the Italians and they seem to love me back – *what a blessing!* Italians do *everything* with love as the source, which sounds uber corny and cringey, but there truly is no other way to say it. The 'eat' part of the story *Eat, Pray, Love* so perfectly captures this. I feel like I am Elizabeth Gilbert when I am in Italy, experiencing the struggles and wonderment of being *in* this culture – enjoying goat's cheese directly from the source and playing language charades in every exchange. Italians love sharing food, telling interesting tales and welcoming you to their homes and businesses. They are *so direct* it's refreshing; they refuse to hold back their thoughts or feelings and bring passion to everything they do. Passion and pleasure . . . WHATTA LIFE!

Sardinia

You'll never hear me describe a place with more love and delight than Sardinia. This place *is it* for me. I will always go to Sardinia when visiting Italy, for me it's non-negotiable, and spend at least a day on my favourite beach in the world – Cala Mariolu. This alone fills my satisfaction quotient to overflowing.

If the world changed its international travel laws and we could only select one place to visit for the rest of our lives, I would gladly move permanently to Sardinia and make Australia my vacay destination. SARDINIA IS SOMETHING ELSE. Truly. Madly. Deeply. Its own piece of magic. Although technically part of Italy, it's essentially its own country.

There are Italians, then there are Sardinians. While under the same national umbrella, Sardinians are their own kind. Their personalities and produce have drawn me back five times and counting. Each trip I'm determined to discover more, a quest I'm coming to realise may have no end, as the island is filled with endless enclaves of magical energy, food, beaches and people, most of them middle-aged to elderly. In fact, the absence of young people on the island is so dire that at the time of writing the Sardinian government is offering €15,000 to move there, with the hope of attracting younger generations. Nonetheless, Sardinians are passionate about their island and committed to keeping their long-standing traditions alive – and I can absolutely see why. To sample the taste of freshly grown vegetables from a Sardinian farm will single-handedly become one of your most memorable taste experiences – a delicacy grown by the gods.

How to get there

To get to Sardinia, you fly (50 minutes) or catch a ferry (8 hours) from Naples. Since the price difference between the two is around €60, I don't think the ferry is worth the lost time or inconvenience but, hey, you do you. Once you land, I recommend you hire a car. While there are trains and buses that travel through the major cities, they do miss major parts of the island. So, if you are confident and able, drive yourself.

If, like me and every other Australian, you drive on the opposite side of the road, then it's best to take the car straight from the airport onto a highway toward a smaller town, far from the chaotic drivers. If that's the case, best you save the cities of Alghero and/or Olbia for the last few days on your way back, after you've dropped the car off. While the traffic in Alghero and Olbia is not as bad as Rome and Naples, it is moving, shaking and happening, so in my opinion, best avoided.

The direction I take the car depends mainly on one thing: where I have booked my accommodation. Normally I will have prebooked a few cute-as-pie Airbnbs across the island, leaving huge gaps in between. This allows me the certainty of seeing some specific places I've planned to visit with enough time to move around loosely. Sardinia is not an island *where everything is booked* so you can relax; if you have a car in tow, you can go anywhere. If there is no accommodation in one town, you will find more in the next. I can wholeheartedly confirm this, so relax your little control-freak heart and lean into the experience of loose travel.

I have found that a three-to-four-day stint in one area is the best amount of time as it gives you several opportunities to head in different directions so you can

experience the region's various beaches, restaurants and other highlights. Having only one or two days feels rushed and anywhere more than five is too long. Beyond my prebooked accommodation, I use Google to search other areas and will randomly choose a place I like the look of that fits the budget. I let my love of aesthetically beautiful spaces dictate my bookings and am yet to be failed by this process.

For a connected experience with locals, book a B&B, best done via Booking.com as most places don't have their own website. These overly generous hosts will care and shower you with good energy as if you were part of the family. Their breakfast bars alone are worth the journey, filled with nonna-made breads and treats including the most superb local yoghurt and fresh fruit. It's these enriching connections with the locals that will woo you back to Sardinia to discover more year after year, no doubt.

Where to go in Sardinia
Land in Olbia and get a car, drive to the beach Porto Istana and get some sunshine, snacks and beach time.

Drive to the region of Dorgali and book somewhere to stay for three to four days. This region of Sardinia is my FAVOURITE. Best beaches in the world. Over your stay visit Cala Fuili, Cala Liberotto, Cala Osalla beaches. Ignore the cringey name, but Wikipizza in Dorgali serves a delicious meal.

After Dorgali, head south to a small town called Gergei. Last visit I had a REALLY YUMMY meal at the only restaurant in town – gorgonzola pancetta pizza to die for. I can't suggest booking the place because it seemed like a seasonal pop-up, but if you find yourself there, use your nose to sniff out the local delights. Local beaches I think are great are Torre di Bari (there's a really good restaurant on the water called Hotel La Torre – menu is outstanding) and Marina di Tertenia.

I encourage you to continue south to visit the Villasimius, Cagliari and Sant'Antioco areas and explore these parts. My other favourite area and one of my top-three favourite beaches in the world is Spiaggia Corrighias. This is the PERFECT full beach situation as there is ample parking, a restaurant and, without a doubt, the most incredible water you will ever have the pleasure of seeing and feeling.

On the west side of the island, Tresnuraghes has a very cute hotel called Villa Asfodeli with the most perfect pool. The restaurant next door, called Su Palatteddu, serves fresh-caught fish and traditional homemade Sardinian specialities. Visit the beaches Cane Malu and Mandriola.

Next, head north to the little beach town of Bosa. It's cute, FULL of really good food, great beaches and there is a nightlife vibe in the main centres of the town. Try the focaccia from Prodotti Tipici.

Continue north to the beaches Villanova Monteleone, Aglientu and Spiaggia La Pelosa or Stintino. You will have your mind blown at Stintino. I was hosted by the most wonderful family who grew and made all of the food featured at the daily breakfast.

Next, a real gem of a town: Castelsardo. I stayed right on the water and visited the Castelsardo, Porto Torres and Baia Ostina beaches. If you visit Castelsardo then you must visit Elisabetta Milia bakery and order one of everything – thank me later.

Before heading to the airport to leave Olbia, make a dash to Porto Istana for one last aqua dip.

I encourage you to move through Sardinia with loose plans. Visiting smaller towns off the beaten track will gift you the most enriching experience. While the beds might not be the comfiest, you can bet your arse that breakfast will be more than satisfying and the hospitality top-notch. Once you experience the heaven that is Sardinia, you won't be able to set foot in Europe again without hitting your hooves toward its crystal-filled beaches.

GREECE – HOME OF KINDNESS

People, in Australia especially, go on and on and on about Italy and rightfully so – it gets a lot of travel time and conversation time between us and I cannot critique this too hard as my entire business revolves around the Italia pleasures of life. However, I must admit that while my affiliation for Italy is deep, whole and forever binding, Greece has something powerful going on with me.

My obsession with Greek culture has always been on display. When I lived in Brisbane in my early 20s my room was Santorini-themed in Greek blues and whites, including a Greek flag. Though I had yet to visit Greece I'd been inspired by the movie *Mamma Mia!* I have a few close Greek friends in Melbourne and they call me 'sister'. Sprout's nickname is Kouklitsa (cook-lit-sa), Greek for 'cute baby doll'. To this day, if I meet a stranger and they say they are Greek, then BAM! I automatically love them.

Greece is more understated than Italy and that's exactly why I love it. Greeks are equally proud of their country but not as showy with it, or at least that's how I see it. I will always go to Greece after visiting Italy as I enjoy the fresh food shake-up after eating paninis and carbohydrates at every meal. Italian cooking is truly divine, but it does get a little much when you've done it hard for six-

plus weeks. When I arrive in Greece, I am excited to eat souvlaki, Greek salads and beans – literally everything in sight. Greek food hits the spot for me with flavours and freshness and I thoroughly enjoy it, thanks to the simplicity of their cuisine. While not typically a seafood fan, I branch out in Greece because there, for some reason, it tastes different than it does back home.

Greece is vast with endless islands and pockets, which can make the task of choosing where to visit rather overwhelming to say the least. For me, personally, to avoid losing lots of travel days (unless you have four-plus weeks up your sleeve), I'll opt for one area and explore that fully, rather than darting around everywhere. While there are ferries between many of the islands, you can't necessarily travel directly to the ones you want to visit, so you may spend half your day waiting for a connection. Although I'm sure Epicurus and his mates would suggest stopping to try the local yoghurt with honey and Freddo espresso. What are you in a rush for, huh? The beach? It's not going anywhere. *E la?*

There are *soooo* many wonderful pockets of Greece I have explored and still so many to visit. I don't have the space to cover them all, so instead I'm going to home in on the Samos Prefecture, consisting of the island trifecta: Samos, Ikaria and Fournoi Korseon. The latter I have not visited, the other two . . . well, COME ALONG to my Blue Zones heaven and take a tour with me.

Ikaria and Samos

Samos Prefecture comprises three Greek islands that hang together just off the east of Turkey: Samos, Ikaria and Fourni. Ikaria, you have heard of from my obsession with Blue Zones. I was there, writing this book, when I was unexpectedly medevaced to the second and main island, Samos, for surgery. The third is the tiny island of Fourni, just 32 square kilometres and home to around 2,000 inhabitants. It's known for its incredible seafood and tiny port of family-run hotels and restaurants.

These islands are the furthest away from Athens and mainland Greece, and with this comes a slight jolt back in time. As we know from Blue Zones, Ikarians are known for their longevity, their slow methods of doing things and dedication to the simple ways. This is wonderful for people like me who want to immerse themselves into the full cultural experience of zero time constraints and limited internet service; however, if you are searching for well-kept, pothole-free roads, spa parlours and four-star resorts then . . . maybe don't go to Ikaria – no fancy cars, high-flying hotels or Michelin-starred restaurants here. Even the supermarkets, accommodation and restaurant options are slim – and that's okay. Food is slow and home-grown; Ikaria doesn't change for anyone.

If you are coming here to check out a Blue Zone, then please do so respectfully. Your quest on this island should not be to gawk at the oldies and overwhelm them with your questions, rather, to arrive quietly, observe the pace of the island and absorb its energy simply by following how they live. Slow down, grow your food or buy it minimal, spend afternoons on the beach with family, and nights cooking and conversing with mates until the wee hours. No word of a lie, you can still hear people laughing and talking throughout the island until 6 am. Ikarians are notorious for their sunrise bedtimes, due to enjoying last night's company. Sleep when we're dead, huh?

Enjoying Ikaria
My first trip to Ikaria was made special before I even arrived. On the ferry over I struck up a conversation with Athenian lecturer Maria and her husband, Nico, who had a daughter my age. Their family was from Ikaria and they were coming home for the summer. During our chat I shared my travel plans. They suggested I cancel my booking and go with them instead to celebrate the local Paniyiri (Saints' Day) Festival. This is how the Greek 'Gods of Loose Travel' work in your favour! Zeus, is that you? Ikaria is *renowned* for its Paniyiri and after our delicious late dinner we headed to the village centre where we danced, drank and laughed until 3 am. It was one of the most heart-warming, perfect nights of my life, another example of pure *philoxenia* and following your gut on the right people.

If you decide to visit Ikaria, I recommend splitting your time between the north and south side of the island, basing yourself around one of their two ferry ports, Evdilos or Agios Kirikos. In my opinion you absolutely need a car for this place (you'll understand when you see it), so please visit my very lovely and helpful new friend Dimitris at Lemy Rent a Car. When I was airlifted off Ikaria with my rental car on the wrong side of the island, Dimitris was an angel and leaped into gear, not only sorting the car but helping me with anything I needed; you should see the lovely text messages he sent me in hospital. Please give him your business!

You have to spend an entire day at Nas Beach (take snacks) and Seychelles Beach should not be missed, but be prepared to hike down a rocky canyon to get there. Armenistis is a cute little village with a quiet beach and some yummy cafés, Anna's Fish Tavern at Nas Beach is a must-do (even if you don't like seafood!) and the little town of Therma and its thermal pools will warm your toes and heart in equal parts. Ikaria will amaze you with its simplicity and its slowness as you wonder how they manage to be so happy with not a lot going on; and maybe therein lies the genius behind it all.

Places to visit on Samos
I cannot comment as much on Samos as we had a 10-day love–hate affair. However, I did take in a few gems thanks to my taxi driver George who took me sightseeing around the island to lift my mental state after being inside and lying down all day. We stopped at the beaches I wished to swim at but couldn't because of my stitches, and I now have a long list of places to eat at when I return.

Based on my limited experience, if you go to Samos I highly recommend the hotel that saved my soul, Ino Village Hotel. The rooms are *soooooo* nice, the site is beautiful, the pool is a bonus, the staff are heroes and the breakfast alone is worth the booking fee. I would go as far as saying that the breakfast bar was the best I have ever had – the honey, grapes and yoghurt – nothing compares. It's situated right near Samos town and lots of restaurants and bars, but the hotel staff can also organise you a car hire or taxi quick-sticks if need be. On my little day tour, I noted down the following things to revisit again on my own, as they either looked really special or I was told by multiple locals that they were not to be missed:

- Kokkari Beach and village were by far my favourite part of the island and I absolutely will return and stay here.
- Tsabou Beach and Lemonakia Beach will enlarge your eyeballs.
- We walked around the cutest mountain village called Manolates.
- I had one delicious meal out with my Samos saviours, the Margaronis family, at restaurant Ariston. The food was divine, as was the local *vino*, which, contrary to my general thoughts on white wine, did not taste like cat piss.

Samos is a bit more modern than Ikaria, it boasts nicer accommodation, but the same simple living, simple eating, simple loving Greek vibes – something that should not be missed during this lifetime. Much to learn, much to see, much to experience, and many people and teachers still to meet.

The places we venture among bring sweetness to a satisfying life. People and spaces inspire me, especially when I travel. If I'm too long in one place, I need a shake-up in visuals to ignite my next project. The gift I have right now of being single and working for myself, with no ties to a mortgage or particular job prospects, means the world REALLY is my oyster and I feel very conscious of using this gift of freedom while I have it. One day, I hope to travel with my own kids in tow, but right now, enjoying my fifth margarita by the pool comes guilt free. If you're already at the travelling-with-cherubs stage, I hope you can swap some time with your partner or gift it to a friend. Enjoying a day of silence and alone time on far flung shores is something to be cherished.

PRINCIPLE 8
Places

Getting outside your safe space may feel overwhelming and huge, but the gifts of travel and new experiences are worth every step.

Find the sweet spot between working and living – an existence that balances the two.

Put your trust in the unknown and embrace loose travel. With money in the bank, a healthy body and travel insurance, you'll be okay.

Ask yourself

Set yourself an achievable goal for an adventure in an unknown place or space. (Hint: it doesn't have to be grand or remote, just new to you.)

Does your home environment reflect the energy you need to rest, recharge and relax? If not, how can you adjust it?

How might you comfortably test 'loose travel' for the purpose of experience and growth?

Write down 5 places you want to visit. Which one is achievable within 2 years and what are the first steps in getting there?

chapter nine

PAIN

THE TRUEST SOURCE OF GROWTH

Pain can trap you with it in the cold, dark cellar or you can flip it and use it to power a top-floor life bathed in sun. The difference between the people who use it versus those who wallow in it comes down to an ability to identify the purpose of pain – how it contributes to a rich, full life because in life we must experience *it all*. We must feel the dips in the road to enjoy the ultimate highs. When we know that at any point things can change, we put pedal-to-the-metal when sunshine lights our path. None of us is immune to feeling pain, but all of us can decide to elevate from it, regardless of its intensity. Sometimes we must fall apart, in order to fall into place.

'Be a rainbow
in someone
else's cloud.'

– Maya Angelou

THINK AGAIN

Sometimes in life, when pain rears its ugly head, you can find yourself in one of two positions: the helpee or the helper. I believe that your ability to be the latter in a productive way will be determined by how you were treated as the former. We all have the ability to turn a pain cycle into a pleasant one. Like when I broke my ankle during Melbourne's lockdowns.

It's the pandemic and I'm helping out a mate by delivering their veggie boxes around Melbourne. I grab a crate from the back of my van and leap straight onto the kerb, shattering my ankle on impact. I black out momentarily from the pain, but then carry on, hopping on my one good foot to deliver the remaining seven boxes. (I refuse to let a mate down.) I finally haul my sorry arse off to hospital and leave an hour later sporting a sexy moon boot and crutches, under orders to rest my ankle for the next eight-to-ten weeks. Being an active gal, I'm not sure how I'm going to cope . . . even worse – I'm gonna need help to survive. Accepting help from others is not my strong point.

I don't have a choice. Unable to do anything for myself, I am forced to rely on others to fetch groceries, clean my house, do laundry and drop me meals. Collingwood businesses send me food packages, while random strangers who've seen my woes via Instagram hand-deliver homemade cookies and lasagne. Neighbours walk my dog, Sprout, and mothers of friends bake me fresh sourdough delivered with bottles of homemade kombucha. Their love and gifts are humbling and I am incredibly grateful.

Soon, my Week 8 check-up rolls around and the doctor confirms my worst fears:

my ankle has frozen and I'm up for another month-long moonboot journey. In despair, I book a few nights at a hotel in Melbourne. If I am going to enter hell I may as well do it with room service, a really comfy bed and ensuite all on one level.

At around 11 am the next morning, a friendly male cleaner arrives to fluff up my room and change things over. I always feel *very uncomfortable* just sitting there while others clean up around me. I either want to make them coffee, or at least help gather *my* shit. However, my inability to move about with crutches means I am unable to assist this time, so I think maybe a good conversation is something I can provide.

Initially, he keeps his replies to a polite minimum, but as I purposely push to generate conversation, he eventually realises I'm keen to chat. As I'm completely *unable* to ever tolerate surface-level conversations, I get straight into the hard-hitting stuff, with the option to, 'Tell me to shut up if you want to!' After 10 or so minutes, I learn that due to the pandemic, his hours have been reduced, his wife's been laid off and, thanks to their residency status, they're unable to access government grants. He is trying to support his entire family – twin boys with learning disabilities about to start high school and needing all the new gear that comes with it – on just two-to-three shifts per week. While anxiety and fear are written all over his face, he continuously expresses his gratitude for being in Australia and his belief that 'everything will work out' – a faith built upon his Hindu practice.

During our conversation he mentions the name of the boys' new school. Once he leaves, I call the school and get a list from the receptionist of the general expenses a child would incur when starting there. After adding them up, I hobble down to the ATM and withdraw the required amount of cash. When I check out the following day, I leave it in an envelope downstairs at reception for him to collect with these words scribbled on the back: *For school uniforms, books and anything else they need. Lovely to have met you! J x*

I thought I had been brought down by my ankle, but this guy's perspective on life shifted my view. My so-called hardship – asking mates for help – was nothing.

No matter how fast we run from pain, none of us will ever be able to escape it, and sometimes it's the most unlikely of folk who zoom in and alleviate the pressure choking us, from a business owner with a broken ankle to a father worrying about his family, and everything in between. Sometimes in life you will notice a friend or a stranger gasping for a breath or a break from their worries, in the same way that you've done at another time. If you're able to provide that breath to them without taking oxygen from yourself, do it. Kindness is a revolving door.

fuck the haters!
you're not the jackass
whisperer.

Brené Brown
dare to lead
How can I have
more courage
be more

RESILIENCE

It's hard to say thanks in a time where we want to say FUCK YOU, because we need to blame something to make us feel better. However, if we learn to understand the reason for the shitstorms and the lessons they teach us, we will search for the rainbows in the midst of the clouds.

I remeber the first time I heard Oprah say that *even* (perhaps, especially) in times of shitness we must say 'thank you' to the Universe. At the time, I thought she was nuts. WHY WOULD I SAY THANK YOU FOR A HORRIBLE TIME when I am not enjoying myself in the slightest and am certainly NOT grateful for it?

I find myself in more stressful situations than the common person, mainly because I take a lot of risks . . . which comes with a lot of problems. Why, you ask, do I keep putting myself through it? Over the years I've learned that as you move through each storm you find yourself at the other end surviving, maybe not thriving, but nonetheless stronger than you were before that first droplet of stress hit your head. My achievements and the wonderful events that have taken place in my life certainly have taught me things; however, it's the trials, tribulations and times of utter fucked-ness that have impacted me *the most* and caused *the most* change. It might have taken me a while to jump onboard, but these days I say thank you even when I don't want to – even when I want to torch the Universe and become a non-believer.

Resilience is the capacity to recover quickly from difficulties – a level of toughness. If you are entering the world of owning a business then you must call on resilience to guide you through, as difficulties will drop on you by the bucketful. Without sounding too egotistical, I can say I have *truly* dealt with some disasters that would have well and truly annihilated most people. Somehow, I have always come back. Never let the bastards get you down, I say.

I have heard at least 54,083 times from mates, 'Man, if only people could see what's happening BEHIND THE SCENES in the PM world – sheeeesh, Mama!' It's A LOT sometimes, but I wouldn't trade it for anything because all my risks have fast-tracked me to where I am now. In those times of getting back on the biz saddle after being violently and unexpectedly bucked off, Mama Holmes dubbed me the Persian Warrior Princess. So just for you, here is a resilience story to top them all, an experience that still gives me shivers when I think about it and I *truuuly* cannot believe we lived to tell the tale. Buckle up.

We had spent the previous weeks renovating a beautiful little courtyard to hold our first in-person Pasta Clubs, post lockdowns. We had a full two-week run of hot-shit smaller Christmas parties booked for the staff of Mecca, Westpac and Afterpay, as well as some other Melbourne small businesses. Needless to say, the next fortnight would be exciting but also VERY large and pressure-filled, especially in a new space and presenting our experience to a commercial crowd, not just some fun-loving followers.

The weekend before these parties were to take place we planned a small 'Bye Bye Melbourne' Pasta Club for our friends, Zoë and Hamish Blake. They had tried my red sauce over lockdown and were keen to experience it in person before leaving Melbourne to live in Sydney. Being our first event, albeit a practice run before the corporate events, it felt very pressured. I knew their foodie friends would be in attendance casting judgement on my laissez-faire affair.

As if my anxiety had called in the ultimate shit-to-hit-the-fan, I fell down the stairs the night before, injuring my other ankle badly. At least I owned crutches! I had to beg my left-hand lady, Asti, to do the food running and my friend Hana to make the drinks. No problem, we had it sorted . . . or so we THOUGHT. Then the chef called in, cancelling two hours before the event, literally minutes before Zoë texted me a picture of her Zimmerman outfit ready and raring to go.

DEATH BE UPON ME . . . HOLY FUUUUUCCCK WHAT AM I GOING TO DO??

I know in this situation most people would cancel. But I cannot cancel! I actually can't, it's not an option. If I ever cancelled a Pasta Club it would be because some *serious shit* had occurred. I will not disappoint people if I can avoid it in any way. I would rather serve 6-out-of-10 food than cancel, because cancelling would give them a nothing experience and 100 per cent disappointment, which can be hard to come back from.

After panic dialling the inner sanctum, some friends begged me to call it off saying it wasn't worth the stress cooking for the first time in this setting and others said: 'Well. . . if anybody can do it, it's YOU JHo.' In the end, we landed on the only option: *I would have to cook.* Not only for Zoë and Hamish, but LORD KNOWS WHO THEY WERE BRINGING. Was well-known Kiwi chef Ben Shewry, a good mate of theirs, turning up? Fuck me, what about some *Vogue* food critic? I CANNOT HANDLE THIS LEVEL OF STRESS. Well . . . too late, it's happening.

Prior to this, every Pasta Club had relied on chefs and while I'm a handy cook among friends, I had yet to professionally prepare food for 16 people. Nonetheless, my daily mantra is: *I am capable. We shall persevere*. So, we did. With my sprained ankle, I somehow whipped up the eight dishes by relying on recipes I handwrote using the ingredients I had available (telling myself I would deal with my mental health at a later point). I'll admit, I fucked up the pesto gnocchi for the vegan *so badly* I still wanna vomit when I think about it. That said, vegan gnocchi is hard and I was so terribly overwhelmed in that kitchen I might have blacked out the experience, to be honest.

Finally, I went out to the dinner tables and cleared dessert, only then letting them know that since the chef had cancelled last minute, yours truly had just cooked for them all. Thankfully, this was met with genuine shock which perfectly matched how I felt. It was as if I'd just been smacked across the face, but had yet to process it. Thankfully everyone was happy, so from then on, with a few adjustments, I cooked for every Pasta Club for the next year and a half, until I once again started hiring other female chefs. Phew . . . but, the resilience story does not end here, folks.

After our little fun on the Saturday night, the neighbours got annoyed and sent me this text:

Hey just letting you know there is not an active liquor licence on the place next door so if you have anything on this week, you need to sort alternative licensing.

SHUT. THE. FUCK. UP. Since Saturday had been a non-commercial dinner for friends, there'd been no problem there, but my upcoming events were a different story. You can only imagine the phone call from me to our venue mates. When we'd signed the place, they'd agreed to manage the liquor licence and had assured me it was all in hand. In the following week, we had three events booked for Thursday, Friday and Saturday, two with Mecca and the other with Westpac, each their *first* staff get-together post lockdown . . . so the excitement and pressure was hectically real. As I began calling my contacts to try and get ourselves covered in time, I had to decide whether to proceed with one last remaining friends' event. With no licensed venue in place, the only option was to host it at home. The last thing I wanted to do was annoy the neighbours before the big events began.

Refusing to cancel on and disappoint my mates, I fell upon standard P Mami distress activation – calling everyone I knew to see if they could help me transform my front studio into a restaurant and drag over all the furniture, plants, plates, cups, cutlery and things from the other P Club location, in order to pull it off there instead. I distinctly remember packing plates into boxes while stress-crying as four of my mates left their jobs at lunchtime to move all the furniture into my house so we could set up P Club for 20 guests. I arrived home to a friend cleaning my toilet and mopping my floors (true friend!) and set about in sheer panic, dressing the tables as I moved between rooms.

Once again, we survived and my guests had an awesome time. Sure, it would have been easier to cancel on them and not push through what was *beyond hard* mentally and physically. But, what I realised in choosing resilience was that my reputation would be upheld – worth so much more than pushing through a few hard hours. Yes, our guests could have had a pub meal down the road and I could have saved myself a few grey hairs and wrinkles; however, they were expecting to have a Pasta Club experience and so, we would give them one.

While cleaning the dishes and wrapping up Thursday's event, the Universe repaid us. We received a temporary licence to cover our events for the next two weeks. HALLE-FUCKING-LU-JAH-HEY! It felt as if my commitment and resilience had been rewarded. When everyone else wants to run away and shut things down because it's easier, I put my cap on, gather my mates and run straight in. I refuse to do anything but my best and if my best means cooking on a sprained ankle or begging loyal friends to leave work to turn my house into a restaurant, then we do whatever it takes.

HOW TO EXECUTE AN IDEA – P MAMI STYLE

By now I have mastered the art of my idea cycle – a specific set of stages that unfold at different rates depending on the size and timing of an idea. The ideas I have transformed into streams of income have made it because I constantly checked in on my current stage of the idea cycle and applied past knowledge to determine whether to keep going, pause or kill it. Please note that this is my personal idea ladder which you may want to switch around depending on your idea, industry and experience.

> Every idea is a good idea until proven otherwise.

The greatest lesson to be learned from this cycle is failure – our mightiest teacher who should never be feared. *Eighty per cent of my ideas have failed*. The only reason the other 20 per cent have succeeded is because of the failed 80 per cent and what I learned from them. Motto? Work as if it will succeed, but don't explode when it doesn't. Innovation demands failure, so the sooner you make peace with it, the faster you will improve.

The key to successfully moving through these stages is that you must always be in data collection-and-reflection mode. Constantly check in, asking yourself: 'How are people reacting to this?', 'How much effort does this need to continue and do I have it?' and 'Am I getting closer to the final result?'

Stage one – write it out

Get the idea out of your head and onto paper. Sometimes the brain can skew how wonderful an idea is, so laying it all out will give you the chance to assess its plausibility. From the scribbles, pull out some key words or specific parts you know are crucial. Be ready to change parts of your initial plan, but know its key points.

Stage two – budget

Comparing the finances required with what you have in the bank is a surefire way of understanding an idea's prospects. Turning ideas into reality costs money – sometimes a lot, sometimes a little. The critical question to ask yourself at this stage is: 'How much money can I give to testing this idea without affecting my current financial needs too much, and am I willing to lose that amount if it does not work out?'

If an idea is going to immediately sink all your finances, DON'T do it.

Stage three – research

This stage allows your idea to take form by assessing the following:

- Does this idea already exist? If it does, who is executing it and how are they doing it?
- Am I able to contribute something differently? What gap will I be filling?
- What do all the elements cost? Google potential suppliers to get a range of costs and understand the finances required to start phase one of your idea.
- What are the legal requirements surrounding your idea and bringing it to fruition? Consider contracts, insurance, etc.
- What method will you use to share your idea with people. Digital, in-person, other? How will the consumer receive it?

Stage four – the task of the ask

Your greatest asset in business is the *task of the ask.* There is nothing more valuable than getting feedback straight from the horse's (consumer's) mouth! Why slog at something you 'think' people need, only to find out you're the only one excited by this 'gap in the market'?

People enjoy being queried about their opinion and I have received an endless stream of valuable insights simply by running my 'great idea' past select people. To be of any use, they should either reside within the target market of your idea to help you identify its needs, or give you another perspective on your idea. Of course, all feedback should be taken with a grain of salt!

Stage five – create and test

Based upon your research about what the market needs, create the first physical prototype of the idea (also called 'proof of concept' or 'minimal viable product'). An idea will have many cycles of change in the beginning, with each cycle costing time, finances or both. Using low-risk tests will ensure you can make those changes without causing too much trouble. Allocate a limited amount of cash from your budget to create something that allows you to dip your toe in the market and test it with low risk. You want to find the balance between creating enough of the idea so that people can test it and give you feedback, while not so much it can't be changed or altered based upon that feedback.

Stage six – feedback and iterate

The feedback and data from testing will help you identify a couple of things. Firstly, sales are a great indicator of interest as numbers do not lie. Secondly, people's engagement, attitude and energy toward your idea will be clear upon experiencing it – watch this closely. Assessing your idea's *usefulness* in the world will inform adjustments in the early stages. If your idea runs cohesively and people love it, then keep going. If people love it, but there are a few kinks that will affect their desire to engage with it in the future, then continue to change it until those kinks are ironed out.

This is the perfect time to do an 'idea check-in' with yourself, assessing your available financial and time commitments for executing the next testing phase. If you find yourself with an exhausted budget alongside data that points toward this idea *not* filling a gap, then ever so proudly and slowly walk away. No idea is worth your physical and mental health – this much I know is true.

FAILURE, RISKS AND EXPENSIVE LESSONS

Every idea is a good idea until proven otherwise. All have space to exist in thought, and validity in their purpose. This notion gives me the freedom to try everything at least once. If it works, great. If not, on to the next thing. The faster I work, the faster I can fail – and the sooner I can move on to the next thing. Not all ideas will be birthed, let alone make it onto the page of consideration. My idea to create a border collie habitat on an Italian island is not likely to be realised, but it's oh-so-nice to think about it in my head. Great ideas will always break through the surface, leaving the bad ones behind in their wake.

Of course, if the risk of failure is potentially much worse than landing back at square one, maybe it's time to reconsider. Not every idea deserves to get breath; sometimes they can just be fluttering thoughts that have no realistic purpose or ability to be birthed by you – they just risk too much. Dragging an idea beyond its expiration date can drown you in financial and time stress, which is why constantly checking in is a sure way to safeguard against ultimate doom.

The skill of identifying whether an idea has legs is developed through trial and error. When you accept your idea pilgrimage you also accept its inevitable roadblocks. No idea hunter is exempt from them – they're specifically laid out to test you. And just when you think you have removed the obstacle from the road, another bigger, heavier one pops up. These roadblocks exist to test your determination – what you're willing to put up with to see the idea out. Sometimes the roadblocks get cleared by the solutions you throw at them. At other times, no crane, money or community of people can help move that damn thing, so you gather your things and walk away.

The walk-away can be the hardest act, especially after time, money and energy have been funnelled into an idea. A walk-away or an idea failure can naturally produce an element of shame and embarrassment, as we live in a society that expects nothing but achievement. Failure has been so intrinsically linked to feeling 'wrong' that we have forgotten that it's actually the fastest route to success.

Great ideas will always break through the surface, leaving the bad ones behind in their wake.

Failure has been so intrinsically linked to feeling 'wrong' that we have forgotten that it's actually the fastest route to success.

Even apparently successful ideas still face their own failures and roadblocks. Pasta Club is a successfully running idea, yet we fail at something AT LEAST once a week. Let me share ONE ICONIC WEEKEND OF FUCKEDNESS:

Friday: Had a big public Melbourne P Club and the chef called in sick TWO HOURS before service and I had to personally call every person and cancel . . . while I was cooking for 50 people in Sydney. Literally cutting onions and crying – not from the onions – as I called everyone and apologised.

Saturday: Went to an event and the kitchen equipment we rented didn't work. People were waiting for their food so we bought camping stoves from Bunnings, just so we could feed everyone.

Sunday: Instead of 160 shallots, 168 bunches of spring onions arrived for a Pasta Club at Home catering job. BIG FUCKING DIFFERENCE. But whatever; we figured it all out.

I do not believe we will be exempt from hard times, ever. The roadblocks do not become less scary or less stressful the more you face them. What changes is the rate at which you are able to implement effective solutions and your ability to apply past experiences to future choices and changes. The idea horse will kick you off its damn saddle many a time and you can either gather your things and leave the stable or choose bravery and jump right back on.

My number-one piece of advice when accepting the call to work with an idea is to ask yourself this very important question: 'If this all fails, what is the worst that can happen?' Then, 'What will happen if it succeeds?' and finally, 'How might this idea contribute to my life?'

Most people, including myself, if asked about the worst outcome regarding their idea, would answer something like this: 'Well, the worst situation would be that I lost a bit of time and money, but mainly I would just be embarrassed that it did not work. Then I would just come back and work where I am now: *square one*.'

> Better to have moved forward in fear than not to have moved at all.

Square one. Not something people should be afraid of. Sometimes square one is the *best* place to be. You recoup, regroup, reflect and absorb all the learnings you gained while jumping between squares two and five. So even if you are technically back on the grid at square one, yours is a new version – bigger, more developed, more aware. Experience cultivates experience. Better to have moved forward in fear than not to have moved at all.

As you play this game, you'll start to recognise the signs indicating which ideas have the potential to grow legs. You'll be able to decide more quickly whether to 'toss' or 'keep' the concept. Anyone can *have* a great idea, but who can actually *action* it effectively?

To co-pilot the quest of bringing a wonderful and *useful* idea into fruition is one of life's most wonderful experiences. And fruit is better from a regularly pruned tree, so be okay with cutting off mediocre ideas so that sweeter and juicier ones can flourish.

EXPENSIVE LESSONS

I have taken an unconscionable amount of risks. Truly, madly and deeply. With their never-ending stream comes a multitude of outcomes and while you can meticulously plan for all of them, life will still shit on you and on your business goals in the blink of an eye. Through all of my explosive business disasters and personal struggles, I have remained focused on the light at the end of the tunnel, which has been to create a life where I can execute my creative ideas around fun people while slowly becoming the best version of myself along the way. I think I am doing that . . . I feel like I am doing that . . . and the closer we all come to arriving at a place where we are working in alignment with our soul's purpose, the nicer the general vibe of the world will be.

Of the many things my mum has taught me, this might be one of the best. Whenever I would call her to share my woes, she would soothe my angst with, 'It's okay, Mays, it's just another expensive lesson.' Expensive lessons are exactly what they sound like: lessons that *cost you a lot*. Whether in money, time, effort, energy or something else, they drain you of important resources. Like the time I was told to 'not touch the boxes' after an event and I did, in fact, touch the boxes, instantly dropping one that contained $2000 worth of breakables I had to replace. This is why I was told not to touch the boxes – we all knew that my butter fingers in conjunction with glass vases was set to deliver me an expensive lesson.

The key word, though, is 'lesson'. If we refuse to take new understanding from the shit scenario, it *truly is* a waste because we set our future selves up to experience the painful 'expense' once more. This is how people fail to grow. Sometimes the lessons have to be expensive in order for you to take notice, as if their seriousness is the only thing that will make you pay attention and act differently the next time around. At least, that's what happens to me.

I sometimes need to be hit right between the eyes in order to hear it – the most loud, the most clear, the whole sha-bang. But don't we all? I know some of you out there need it loud too, I refuse to believe I am the only one.

ELPs

Then there are Expensive Lessons People, or ELPs. They teach us the biggest lessons of all: the ones found between the human experience of two souls. ELPs aren't necessarily bad people (although there are some); we are all them at some stage. I am damn sure I have been an ELP for a few people, and you will have been one for someone else, too. It feels to me that it's impossible to live a life without encountering some form of challenging human interaction – a previous partner, a boss or colleague, family or friends, coaches or teachers, even a stranger in a car yelling at you to DRIVE BETTER. The human experience will lay out ELPs on your journey, no matter who you are, no matter how kind you are, no matter what good you do – you are bound to experience an encounter with another person that shatters you, and then some, and then some . . .

Much like expensive lessons, ELPs only weigh you down if you learn nothing from them. Your own ELPs will teach you far more about yourself than your friends or loved ones ever can. It's these strenuous and gruelling relationships that make us strong as we learn to identify our contributions and the impacts of the relationship. Within this reflection we can also learn to detect upcoming ELPs, using our past experience and intuition to determine their potential. While we aim to avoid calling ELPs into our lives, we will inevitably be graced by their presence at some stage. How fast you are willing to take the lesson and apply it will determine how many more lessons you are served.

I lost a good friend because our maturity and experience was not developed enough at the time to realise that two people with different creative processes/styles shouldn't have to change their uniqueness for anything. Better to have walked away from being in business together than destroy our friendship over it – well, that was a lesson I learned the hard way. The other major lesson I've learned, which has been worth its weight in 24-carat gold, was developing the clear understanding that I work best alone, in charge and in control of my creativity, with assistance and support on the side – and only doing so when the feeling's right.

WITH PAIN COMES GROWTH

Pain allows past moments of pleasure to be appreciated and future moments to be desired and feel even sweeter when they come. Have you ever had a long bout of ill health, bedridden for four months sipping instant coffee made with lacklustre oat milk? When you finally muster the strength to walk to your local café, your espresso tastes *bellissima* – trust me, I've been there. The little things become big things by their absence.

As much as we would prefer it, life cannot only be about things that make us feel good – it's the challenges that form a person. Character and courage are built in tough times, not consuming fresh cherries and cream on a daybed by Lake Como. While it is important to have pleasure, it doesn't call forth transformation and transcendence. Welcome your friend pain, knowing that pleasure is lurking around the corner and will arrive soon enough, once you've worked through this raincloud.

Without pain, I wouldn't be where I am today. I've had huge successes and even larger failures: $1.43 in the bank account one week and $52K the next, great employees and soul-destroying ones, awesome clients and fuckheads that could have sent me to jail from wanting to – arghhh! – if my friends hadn't held me back . . . The list goes on. I am acutely aware that my lessons are still coming and I am 98 per cent sure I have a business lesson brewing right now which will arrive to kick my butt in a few hours' time.

Right at this moment, I am riding a new wave of hectic business predicaments as I continue to expand my company. Beyond my capacity to handle alone, they will be solved with the help of others. I know, if I continue, things will get bigger and hairier across all fronts, leaving me no choice but to continue doing what works best: learning, absorbing, reflecting, changing and going again. As each uncomfortable situation subsides it leaves a figurative scar – evidence of a stronger you who will handle the next wave even better.

Painful experiences teach you, no doubt. Personal growth and business growth go hand in hand; you can't have one without the other. Though at the time, I wanted to shrivel up and die when faced with cancelling those Pasta Clubs, I knew deep down I was being driven to embrace the challenge and learn. Those events forced me to take a new – now central – approach to Pasta Club: me cooking.

Try resilience and see what happens. There are fantastic gifts on the other side. I promise.

The storms have their purpose and you can try to run away and hide or you can grow a pair of balls, show up and hold on. The demands of business are a constant test, tempting you to quit 100 times over. Staying in the ring is your choice. Though you can't call the shots, you pull on your boxing gloves and smack yourself in the head for a pump-up, preparing to take on the next round of body blows. Staying upright requires being actively and consciously aware of the steps you are taking – how are you showing up to this? How can you improve your reactions and responses? Are you checking in with yourself on each project and asking if the intention is still clear and on track?

If you are working hard to create a life where you eliminate all pain then I am sorry, my friend, you are chasing a false narrative. There is pain in being disappointed and pain in being disciplined; every action holds pain potential and there's no point running away. If taken as a gift, pain can help us set boundaries to prevent dissatisfaction and to identify our zones of discomfort. It helps us locate the fine line between walking into what's uncomfortable for the purpose of growth and not stupidly entering into something that could smack us unconscious.

Pain's driving force is powerful – it makes us crazy and pushes us further, sometimes for better and sometimes for worse. Never hath an email been written with more fire than a creative responding to someone questioning their value, I tell ya that much. Sometimes I have been so pissed at a client I have gone over and above to deliver, just to spite them. How ironic that on those nights, the pasta is beyond supremo.

I can also attest to a sick kind of satisfaction that comes from surviving the pain. It's usually on the most extreme of stressful nights that I'm served a 2 am boost of adrenaline and dopamine on the drive home. My mouth drops as I conceptualise the fact I have survived – I've endured the wildest shit and am somehow still together as one person. Alive. With no harm. A business that's intact. And clients that are happy.

Over many rounds in the ring, I've learned it is possible to withstand adversity, and that, believe it or not, you are more likely to grow as a person in the midst of it. I have used my ability to adapt, persist and change where I can, granting me a thick skin as I tackle the next blow. Try resilience and see what happens. There are fantastic gifts on the other side, I promise.

I certainly don't have it all figured out – and I think the key is knowing you never *really* figure it all out anyways. You end up searching for some giant thing only to realise that managing multiple paths to find it was the reason for the adventure in the first place.

If I can leave you with two final things to consider as we part ways, at least until next time . . . First, you need not be rich or well connected to experience, on a daily basis, the simple pleasures the world has to offer. Denying yourself this gift is a waste of a lifetime. Close your eyes and savour your next peach, swim at the beach for an extra hour, play your favourite song to a friend, eat your work lunch with your face to the sun, read something from someone you admire, travel to the next town for their best bakery treat. These are the simple things that feel like big things and when we fill ourselves up with big things that cost very little but give us double back, we can take on the world.

Second – and final thought. Whatever looks the hardest, is holding you back, is resistant and feels insurmountable, is normally the thing you need to run directly toward in order to graduate to the next level of growth. It's up to you to determine if you're willing to seek out what's best *in you* and *for you*. Carry under each arm some courage and blind faith that things will always arrive exactly where they are meant to be.

In the end, it's about moving closer toward a you that feels easiest – your strongest self. The one that wakes every day knowing there is no mask to put on or task incoming you cannot face. We are capable, we shall persevere and . . .

This too shall pasta.

This too shall pasta.

WORK AS IF
IT WILL
SUCCEED
BUT DON'T
EXPLODE WHEN
IT DOESN'T.

PRINCIPLE 9
Pain

The sooner we accept pain as a part of our life experience, the sooner we can cultivate the skills of dealing with it constructively.

Work as if it will succeed, but don't explode when it doesn't. Failure is the fastest route to success. Ya gotta lose to win, baby!

Instead of being distracted by, running from, or avoiding what's painful or uncomfortable, embrace it head on, knowing the Universe will direct you in order to protect you.

Soak up everything pain can teach you, but don't let it be the driver of your life.

Ask yourself

Understanding that pain creates growth, how have you seen this unfold in your life?

How do the people around you support you when you are experiencing pain?

Name a time you have been most resilient. How did you feel afterwards?

What have you learned from expensive lessons and Expensive Lessons People? How have they helped you grow?

Name a failure that ended up a winning result.

the
tide
always
changes

EPILOGUE: EAT THE SPAGHETTI TO FORGETTI YOUR REGRETTI

When I was approved to fly and make my way home from Samos to Australia after my operation, I was sad my trip had been cut short but knew in my heart I would be back the following year. There was something special there on that island and it called me to explore it further. Samos had got into my bones.

Once back in Melbourne, the first thing I did was book into a range of health professionals for body, mind and spirit. I had experienced medical trauma and wanted to knock it on the head to avoid any future anxieties around hospitals or doctors. I've always embraced a multitude of approaches when it comes to these things, across both scientific and spiritual practices, so I booked several appointments including therapy, dermatology, kinesiology and reiki. Of these, my reiki energy healer, Magic Melinda, is *always* my favourite appointment, as the most wonderful and accurate revelations come out of her sessions.

We started our appointment and I jumped straight in, telling her about my Samos experience and how confused I was feeling about it. If the Universe really did have my back, I asked, why did it bring my dream trip crashing down?

Over my life of knowing her, Melinda has often given me shivers as my energy aligns with the thing she is saying. But her explanation of Samos might go down in history as one of the most resonant moments between us: pure clarity, reason and explanation. Her words blew my mind and changed my entire outlook on life.

As she began speaking, I felt the shivers begin. I've told this story many times since, and seen the same thing happen to others, time and again. When Melinda first imparted her insights, I was reluctant to share them with anyone. I wanted to keep her answer close because it felt so big and true, but it sounded so *unbelievable,* I was afraid of people's reactions. I thought they'd be like, 'Oh boy, P Mami has well and truly lost the plot.' But . . . since you and I know each other well enough by now and you know I'm all for the big A for Authenticity, here it is.

When Melinda spoke, I knew with every inch of my being that what she said was the truth. It was the only possible answer and felt nothing but 100 per cent right. She started by reminding me, 'So, you know how you always joke that you were either a nonna or a *yiayia* in a past life because of your affiliation for all things Mediterranean?'

'Ummm, yeah?'

'There is a reason for that – your instinct about it and all of this.' She paused as if to receive more specific information to share. 'All of this happened because it was always part of the story.'

She paused again. At this point, I just wanted her to get on with it.

'You are correct. You *were* a *yiayia* in a past life.'

I-FUCKIN-KNEW-IT!! Wait. Whaaat? Pause. What did she just say?

'You were born in Samos and lived there – had a husband, family, grandkids, the works. And then you died. In that hospital, due to malpractice.

'The hospital staff ignored you and you were too physically weak to stand up for yourself because you were in your late 90s, so you passed away in the same bed that you, Jenna, were in this time round. The spot next to the window.'

Nope. I *never* told Melinda anything about any window and she does not have Instagram. There is no way she could have known this detail.

'You were an adored member of the Samos people, and the kind strangers in your hospital room, the hotel staff and the familiar homeowners that helped you during this experience innately knew that you were a part of their community from the past. Your cooking intuition and skills you use in Pasta Club come from this Past You and the reason that you are so connected to the island of Ikaria and Blue Zones is because they are literally in the zone – right next door. You have lived and breathed this way of life, that's why it feels so easy and real for you to slip into. As if your true self relaxes the most in that area.'

Oh my god, I *do* love Blue Zones. Ever since that Oprah show . . .

'It's all linked. Past You was incredibly powerful in her decisions and continuously backed herself while maintaining grace – something you needed to bring back.'

Check. I *do* feel more at ease since going through and surviving that hell, so 'grace' is what we're gonna call it? Okay, I can roll with that. Multiple friends had even noticed a change in my state since returning to Melbourne – as if I'd become more calm somehow.

'You were meant to go to that hospital and close the past-life loop by standing up to the doctors. You needed to give something back and to take something with you.'

I definitely felt better after giving those dickheads a serve, that's fo sho.

'There's a lot of important decisions and big things you're going to be doing in this next phase of your life and in your business. In order for them to work out, you first had to take your energy back – through regaining Past You's power and wisdom through this experience.'

More shhhiivvvvveerrrs. Mouth on floor. Eyes popping in shock.

'Let her drive forth those abilities in you,' Melinda says, confidently and calmly. 'You were always going to Samos and to that hospital. It was always a part of the plan in order to set you up for the next phase. Does this make sense?'

Usually, you can never shut me up. Usually – especially with something as epic as this – I'd be bouncing around the walls. I was struck silent. Processing, processing. And then . . .

'OH MY GOD. WOW. Wow. What. Wot. WAT. HOW? Yes. Yeah! Absolutely. Like YES. Definitely! One-hundred-thousand per cent. That is exactly what it is. Man. Shit. Like what? Yes. That's it. Fuck meeeee! Urrghhh! Live for this!'

My body is shivering, tingling, twitching like an ABBA chorus – all body signals pointing to YES! I truly adore these moments of complete alignment, when the real world matches the spiritual reasoning. THE WHOLE THING MAKES SENSE! I felt the confusion melt off my shoulders.

And just to ensure I'm left with ab-so-l-u-t-ely no doubt, Melinda continues. 'Oh, and was there a really kind female doctor or nurse that helped you? She gave you her email address or phone number?'

'HOW DID YOU KNOW THAT?!'

'Well, I know you have been thinking about emailing her to thank her . . . You should do it. The Universe put her there because you needed someone from the hospital staff to show you a glimmer of kindness.'

Tick.

'And . . .'

No, no. Aren't we done yet? I'm ready to be done.

'The last thing I need to tell you is that someone is helping you write the book.'

God damn, don't I wish. I cross my arms. This better be good.

'Just wait a second.' She pauses for what feels like two hours.

'It's a Greek hero who has come into your orbit before. I can't see clearly how, but you will receive a visible sign in a few weeks and you'll need to lean in and let them help you write the book. You have attracted them into your field for the construction of this book so be open to what they have to say. It will be something to do with you and Samos . . .'

I want more details.

'Just keep an eye out. It will show up and be made clear.'

I am so not good at being patient.

'Now, just finally . . . let's get one thing clear. You weren't punished for anything. Nothing bad is happening. It's part of the book, it's part of you understanding the spectrum of human kindness. Like everything, it happened for a specific reason. Your experience allowed you to get back what you needed to use in this lifetime. Just like always, be open!'

After the appointment, I melted for an hour in the shower. I was both overwhelmed and deeply satisfied with this explanation and end result. It was the answer to so much I have wondered about and I felt lucky to have found it.

Two weeks later I am in Byron. I'm lying on the beach reading a book I plucked off my shelf at home – the book I've broadly based Pasta Club on: *Travels with Epicurus*. I've picked it up to give myself a refresher after four or five years away from it. I'm lying there in the sun soaking up all its care-melting goodness and flip open to the first page.

'Epicurus was born on the island of Samos.'

I gasp so loudly that a group of nearby dogs all turn their heads . . . But not Sprout. She's used to this magic shit.

PASTA

(AND OTHER GOOD STUFF)

So, finally! What many of you came for . . . some delightful RECIPES OF PASTA, plus a few extra special things. As per my food–pleasure philosophy, all are easy and fast to make and rely on basic ingredients, often pantry staples. Some are from my family, some I made up, some are from Blue Zones travels and others from the dinner tables of foodie friends. All of them are *delicioso*. Most importantly, they are built on marrying seasonal with simplicity, cooking with love and intuition, and driven by my lazy-girl approach of high quality for low effort to get dinner on the table in under 30 by 6 pm. *Buon appetito*.

P Mami OG Pasta

This was a recipe idea that was a total stab in the dark and was based purely on flavour intuition, and luckily . . . it paid it off! We have served this all across Australia and it always lands so well, a taste sensation of the ultimate P Mami flavour combination: sour, crunchy, creamy and pleasure filled. You can use the balsamic onions and the pangrattato in other recipes as they make the perfect addition to most dishes. Your friends will think this is very fancy of you, but it's very basic and will be a staple throughout the year, as none of the ingredients need to be seasonal.

FOR 4 PEOPLE YOU'LL NEED

6 white or brown onions
1 cup balsamic vinegar (half for roasting, half in the pan)
6 to 8 cloves garlic (half for roasting, half for pangrattato)
1 × 400g packet dried pasta – best is cavatelli, penne, rigatoni or fusilli
1 cup breadcrumbs
1 bunch picked thyme
2 tablespoons butter
2 cups pecorino
a handful of rocket, rinsed
fancy extra: a burrata ball or stracciatella
+ olive oil, salt and pepper

1. Warm your oven to 200 degrees Celsius while you thinly slice your **onions** and place in a bowl, coating with a few glugs of **olive oil**, **salt** and half the **balsamic vinegar**. Give all the ingredients a good stir, then spread across an oven tray covered in foil or baking paper. Press 3 to 4 **garlic cloves** among the laid-out onions. Cook for 20 to 30 minutes until onions are dark and caramelised. Set aside in a bowl.
2. Put a pot of salted water on to boil. Add the **pasta** to the water and follow the packet instructions for cooking time. Remove from the heat and strain *1 minute before* al dente (firm to the bite, *not* soft and gluey). It should be ready just about the time your pan sauce is.
3. In the meantime, dice up the remaining garlic. In a fry pan on medium heat, add a tablespoon of olive oil, the garlic and **breadcrumbs** and cook for the next 4 to 6 minutes, moving the breadcrumbs around with a wooden spoon

so they don't burn. When the breadcrumbs have turned a golden brown, add in the diced **thyme**, salt and pepper and some more olive oil, and cook for another 1 to 2 minutes. Set aside.

4. In a fry pan on medium heat add **butter**, a tablespoon of olive oil, the cooked onions and the remaining vinegar and stir together. Add the semi-cooked pasta to the fry pan with the onions and mix in ½ to ¾ cup of the pasta water in small doses, adjusting as you stir until the sauce is loose but not runny.
5. Simmer until the pasta is al dente (about a minute). Add half the **pecorino**, salt and pepper and mix all together, then remove from heat and place in a large bowl, stirring through half the breadcrumbs.
6. To plate it up, top with the remaining breadcrumbs, pecorino and a handful of **rocket**. Fancy dollops of **stracciatella** or **burrata ball** can be added here too. YUMBO, YUMBO! Enjoy, enjoy!

The juice is always worth the squeeze pasta

What I love about this pasta recipe is that it's found in many forms across different parts of the world. Once you know the basic combination of flavours, you can add any extras you want, changing the recipe based on what's available to you. All the ingredients can be procured from anywhere, even a petrol station, which I have done. I am not reinventing the wheel here, folks, but if you can take the general principles of this recipe then you will never be left wondering what to cook. I have made it in Samos, Sardinia, Melbourne, Toowoomba, New York and everywhere in between. Obviously the fresher and higher quality the products, the tastier it will be, but a solid container of ricotta and a backyard lemon do just fine.

The lemon grail

Any delicious pasta can be created by combining three things: lemons + herbs + cheese/dairy. That's it – I shit you not. You can make so many combinations with this, believe it or not:

lemon + sage + butter
lemon + basil + ricotta
lemon + mint + crème fraîche
lemon + chives + pecorino
lemon + parsley + parmesan
lemon + thyme + feta

FOR 4 PEOPLE YOU'LL NEED

3 to 4 lemons (depending on size)
1 × 400g packet dried pasta – spaghetti, fettuccine, pappardelle is best
herbs as above
dairy as above
+ salt and pepper, olive oil

1. Boil a pot of salted water and add the **pasta** to cook, according to the instructions on the packet.
2. Fry the **lemon** + **sage** + **butter** mix together while your pasta is cooking until the butter is golden brown, then set aside. Every other combination is made by mixing the fresh ingredients into your cooked pasta: **lemon** juice and zest + chopped **herbs** + **cheese** + **olive oil** + **salt and pepper**.
3. When the pasta is cooked, remove from the water and stir through your chosen flavour combination. Garnish with fresh herbs on top.

Roast capsicum pasta

This is a crowd favourite and super easy to make. It's the perfect flavour combination and takes no time to whip up! A BBQ is the best capsicum roasting process, but never fear, an oven or gas top can assist.

FOR 4 PEOPLE YOU'LL NEED

4 red capsicums
1 brown or white onion
1 × 400g packet dried pasta – spaghetti, rigatoni or angel hair is best
4 cloves garlic
2 cups parmesan
1 cup olive oil
+ salt and pepper

1. Put a pot of salted water on to boil. While waiting, coat **capsicums** in oil and place on a hot BBQ to char, rotating every few minutes once each side is dark brown/black. Add the **onion** sliced in half onto BBQ and cook until brown.
2. Once the water has come to the boil, add the **pasta** to the water and follow the packet instructions for cooking time. Remove from the heat and strain *1 minute before* al dente (firm to the bite, *not* soft and gluey). It should be ready just about the time your pan sauce is.
3. Using a blender or food processor combine the cooked capsicum, onion, **garlic**, half the **parmesan**, **olive oil**, and **salt and pepper** and blend to make a smooth sauce.
4. Add sauce into a fry pan on medium heat and add semi-cooked pasta, simmering for about a minute, until pasta is al dente.
5. Serve sprinkled with remaining parmesan.

zesty zucchini pasta

Zucchini makes another heroic appearance in this dish! This is a zesty, fresh and easy pasta to whip up that will make all your guests swoon and ask for more.

FOR 4 PEOPLE YOU'LL NEED

1 × 400g packet dried pasta – casarecce or spaghetti is best
2 large or 4 small zucchini
1 cup olive oil (half to start, half near the end)
1 bunch parsley
2 lemons
2 cups pecorino
+ salt and pepper
chilli flakes (optional!)

1. Place **pasta** into pot of salted boiling water and cook until a minute off al dente, following packet instructions.
2. Slice **zucchini** into ½ cm-thick rounds. Heat a fry pan and add half the **olive oil**. Fry off the zucchini for 5 to 7 minutes, flipping halfway so both sides are cooked to a dark brown.
3. Dice up **parsley**, zest one **lemon** then juice both, and add all this to the zucchini in the pan.
4. When semi-cooked pasta is ready, add to the zucchini pan. Then add a few tablespoons of pasta water, the remaining olive oil and half the **pecorino**. Stir over heat for another minute or so, until pasta is al dente. Season with **salt and pepper** and add your **chilli flakes** here if using.
5. To serve, garnish with leftover pecorino.

Post-Pasta Club Pasta

Normally after sweating and cooking for the masses at Pasta Club I head home all wired up and make myself my own pasta dish to wind down. For some unknown reason (other chefs agree), you cannot eat a meal when you are cooking for others – somehow the stress kills your appetite – but the second you arrive home it's another story.

This is my pantry/fridge classic that never fails me. I always have the basic ingredients on hand and you probably will too. It's simple, unfussy and of course . . . tasty!

FOR 4 PEOPLE YOU'LL NEED

1 × 400g packet dried pasta – spaghetti or fettuccine is best
125g sundried tomatoes
½ cup olive oil (in stages)
½ cup basil pesto
1 cup cheese – parmesan or pecorino
+ salt and pepper, chilli flakes (optional)

1. Place **pasta** into pot of salted boiling water and cook until a minute off al dente, following packet instructions.
2. Dice **sundried tomatoes** and add to a medium fry pan with a tablespoon of **olive oil** and cook for 1–2 minutes.
3. Add **basil pesto**, the remaining olive oil and **salt and pepper** and mix to form a thick sauce.
4. When semi-cooked pasta is ready, add to sauce pan with a few tablespoons of pasta water. Simmer, stirring for another minute or so, until pasta is al dente.
5. Stir through half the **cheese** and plate up. Add remaining cheese on top and optional **chilli flakes.**

Persian Mama's eggplant stew

This is not pasta but it's just as special, classic, heart-warming and an important part of my history. Both my Persian grandmother and my mum are incredible home cooks and I'm not biased about this – my friends agree it's an absolute privilege to be cooked for by Mama Holmes. Her meals are never fancy or over the top, rather, filled with simple flavours and minimal ingredients and always, always, super affordable. Mum could feed 50 people for $200 bucks, guaranteed.

I have used this recipe for years and years. It's easily whipped up and is a stuuunnning crowd pleaser because, minus one topping (which you can easily leave off), it's completely vegan, dairy-free and gluten-free. I always make this for a food-intolerance crew as it hits all the requirements without any loss of taste (often a tough ask in that arena).

I understand some of you will read 'eggplant' and want to vomit. I wholeheartedly understand this – I really do, and I know what has happened! Eggplant can be terrible if not cooked correctly or drained of its water first – mushy with tough skin – and eaten that way it can definitely cause flavour-PTSD. So, one request: please trust me on this recipe! Just make it once and if you don't like it, then send me an email about it – I mean that. The sauce gets absorbed into the eggplant so you barely taste it.

You can thank Mama Holmes aka the OG Plant Mama, Frances, for this one. May her Persian love language be felt by you all!

FOR 4 PEOPLE YOU'LL NEED

2 medium eggplants
2 cups basmati rice
1 cup olive oil
1 large brown or white onion
4 cloves garlic
2 tablespoons cumin
2 tablespoons turmeric (plus another teaspoon for your rice)
2 tablespoons paprika
2 × 400g tins diced tomatoes
½ cup tomato paste
1 bunch fresh chives (or 2 tablespoons dried)
1 cup natural Greek yoghurt or sour cream
half a lemon
+ water and salt (to draw out the eggplant juices)

1. Prepare your **eggplant** – do *not* skip this step! Slice eggplants across the width, into 2 cm-thick circles, then place on a board or tray. Sprinkle both sides with a decent amount of salt and leave for 20 to 30 minutes, or until water has been drawn out of the eggplants.
2. Cook **rice**. Place rice, 6 cups of **water** and a pinch of **salt** into the pot. Bring to a boil without the lid on. When entire surface is bubbly and foamy, place lid on, turn down to low-medium heat and let simmer for 12 minutes. Remove from heat and let rest.
3. Cook eggplant. Once water has beaded on the surface of your sliced eggplant, rinse them clean under fresh running water. Wipe excess water off with a paper towel and place into a hot fry pan with a *generous* amount of **olive oil** (don't be shy here folks, Blue Zones thrive on the stuff and eggplants are thirsty), searing each side for 2 to 3 minutes until brown. Remove from the pan and once cooled, cut each circle into smaller bite-size cubes and set aside.
4. Dice your **onion** and **garlic**, place into a pre-heated fry pan (with another good gulp of olive oil) and cook on medium heat for 6 to 8 minutes until brown and translucent. Then stir in **cumin**, **turmeric** and **paprika** and cook for another minute until spices are fragrant.
5. Add your diced eggplant, tinned **tomatoes** and **tomato paste** and mix together, cooking for a further 10 to 15 minutes until all the flavours have combined.
6. To your cooked rice, add **butter**, a teaspoon of turmeric and some salt and mix together.
7. To serve, place rice in the bottom of a bowl, top with eggplant mixture and sprinkle with chopped **chives**. For added indulgence, add a dollop of **Greek yoghurt** or **sour cream** mixed with chives and some **lemon juice**.

P Mami's chaotic panzanella

There is no cute back story to this one other than it being ABSOLUTELY DELICIOUS AND EXCITING! Like P Mami? Maybe! This salad of mine is a chaotic mix of strange ingredients that are my favourite tastes (personality traits) and while it seems like it has a lot going on, when you taste all of the flavours combined, it is one very tasty, pleasurable, unique and fresh experience that delivers an unexpected wow! Don't judge it until you understand, accept and experience it. You'll leave a bit more open with your taste buds and perhaps be surprised that these things could come together so perfectly. Imperfectly perfect together, just like me!

FOR 4 PEOPLE YOU'LL NEED

500 grams mixed fresh tomatoes: heirloom, truss, cherry, ox heart, Russian – the juicier and more seasonal, the better – no underripe or juiceless tomatoes allowed!
½ cup white wine vinegar
2 to 3 yellow peaches
1 shallot
half bunch fresh basil leaves and/ or mint – you can use both or just one
3 tablespoons olive oil
200 grams burrata balls or torn fresh mozzarella
bread stick
+ salt and pepper

1. Cut **tomatoes** all ways and sizes and place in a bowl, focusing on being uber rustic in your approach (although making sure each part is bite-size). Once in the bowl, use the back of a spoon to smoosh the tomatoes to release some juices, then add some **salt and pepper** and half of the **vinegar** and set aside.
2. Tear **bread stick** into bite-size chunks, drizzle with olive oil and a sprinkle of salt and toast in the oven until crunchy and brown. Meanwhile, slice the **shallot** into thin rounds, cut the **peaches** into thin wedges and prepare the fresh **herbs** by plucking leaves (set aside for use) from stems (chuck in the compost).
3. Add the peaches, herbs (leave a handful aside for garnish), olive oil, shallots and remaining vinegar to the tomatoes and mix together. Plate up tomatoes, top the centre with **burrata/mozzarella** and finish with extra olive oil, basil and salt.
4. Place toasted bread on a plate next to the salad – you can pile salad on top of a bread piece or bite it in between salad munches. Your gluten-free mates can enjoy the salad without.

Jane's wisdom spring salad

We all need a Jane – monumental gifts in our lives, even better when housed in a wonderfully fun human and especially when they are the undercover queen of food. Well, my Jane is not that undercover because everyone in the food scene knows and adores her, but I call her that because she's the genius operating behind the scenes of some of the most incredible recipes, food-porn table lays and dining experiences across Australia. JANEY'S GOT THE JUICE!

On top of that, Jane gifted me one of my life's greatest lessons and truly flipped my business on its head, for good reason. As a self-confessed control freak, I feel I must do everything, even if my 'everything' is not the best for the situation. At times I struggle to step back and let others take the lead which means I am constantly overworked and it also blocks my business growth. Just prior to our 10 millionth Melbourne lockdown I had escaped to the country, but the demand for Pasta Club at Home surged. As I was out of Melbourne unable to direct the work, I was considering not offering the packs despite the huge interest.

I turned to Jane to talk it through. She asked if I had a strong team. I confirmed that I did. 'Well, do it,' she advised, casual and so calm. 'Let go, trust and just BE ORGANISED. Plan for it all!' And so I did, and guess what . . . NOTHING BAD HAPPENED! We successfully delivered 150 packs and it was actually calmer because I was not there running around like a headless chook. We continued the process for the weeks following and Pasta Mama had one of its most successful periods, all with me remote.

This taught me a really important lesson: plan for it all, find the right people, trust them, then let go. To later be able to leave Melbourne and keep my company running as I arrived in Sydney would have never happened if Jane did not teach me this. You can't control everything. If you want to grow, let go.

This salad is a classic Jane salad, gifted to me from her, which has featured at countless tables! Once again, you'll be confused by the ingredients, but again, please TRUST me as it will blow your palate off, no doubt.

FOR 4 PEOPLE YOU'LL NEED

400 grams brussels sprouts
½ bunch chives, diced
1 cup shaved parmesan
2 pink lady apples, cut into matchsticks
1 cup roasted hazelnuts, chopped
6 tablespoons olive oil
1 tablespoon Dijon mustard
3 tablespoons white wine vinegar
+ salt and pepper

1. With a mandolin or sharp knife, shave or thinly dice your **brussels sprouts**, removing and tossing out the bottom core. It's very important to get the brussels sprouts as finely chopped as possible as nothing is grosser than a chunk of uncooked brussels sprout. Place these in a medium bowl.
2. Add your chopped **chives**, **parmesan** and **apple** and mix together.
3. In a jar shake together the dressing of **olive oil**, **Dijon mustard**, **vinegar** and some **salt and pepper**. Pour over salad and mix all together.
4. Add **hazelnuts** and extra parmesan to garnish. Serve up!

kolokythi goat's cheese salad // koh-loh-kee-thee

One thing I adore about the Greeks' approach to food is their ability to turn the simplest things into an explosion of flavours. You'll eat some lettuce with lemon and be like WHAT ON EARTH IS THIS?!! They have nailed the 'fresh and simple' concept and lean on seasonal to be their hero, always knowing: if you can't grow it, then don't eat it.

We have served this salad at many a Pasta Club and it never disappoints. Especially because zucchinis, aka courgettes or kolokythis, are sometimes so tasteless and boring that half the delight in eating this dish is the shock of realisation when this flavour bomb hits your saliva glands and your eyes are like – oh! Zucchini?!! It's fresh, easy and will surprise you with each bite. The key to this dish is to make sure the zucchini is sliced into thin ribbons, not large chunks. You'll understand why when you eat it!

FOR 4 PEOPLE YOU'LL NEED

2 large, or 4 small, zucchini
2 lemons
1 bunch each mint and dill
200 grams goat's cheese or stracciatella
¾ cup roasted hazelnuts
+ salt and pepper, olive oil

1. In a medium mixing bowl slice your **zucchini** length ways so you get long, thin strips. You can use a mandolin or a vegetable peeler; just make sure they are *thin*!
2. Zest half a **lemon** and squeeze all the juice from both halves, then pour the zest and juice over the zucchini ribbons. Add **olive oil**, mix together and set aside.
3. Toast **hazelnuts** in a medium heat fry pan for 3 to 5 minutes until brown. Remove from heat, dice and set aside.
4. Finely chop **dill** and **mint.** Set aside a sprinkle of the herbs for garnish, then add the rest to the bowl of lemon zucchini, along with a pinch of salt and pepper. Mix well.
5. Place the zucchini mixture on a large serving platter, top with dollops of **goat's cheese**, the toasted nuts and herb garnish, a drizzle of olive oil and an extra pinch of salt. ENJOY!

The base: foundational stock

This recipe is essential to a tasty life, our spiritual foundation and the base of our most flavourful selves. My hero Anthony Bourdain had a love affair with a good stock and so do I – it turns the most basic of risottos into wonderful pieces of taste-art, makes any veg plate a Michelin-starred dish and soothes the soul of every great soup ever made.

Forming a base stock is similar to forming a base spiritual practice. Once you have it down pat you can start confidently testing and trying new recipes and experiences with its support, knowing it will back you the entire way. You can use this stock for a multitude of things like risottos, soup bases and gravies and it's fantastic to drink as a bone broth. Even something as simple as boiling your potatoes in broth will take them to the next level.

I use chicken bones in this recipe as they taste the best for me. You can do it two ways: either buy a whole chicken and use the white meat after boiling for salads or soups, or buy just the chicken carcass directly from the butcher (remember to always buy meat from the local butcher rather than supermarkets if you can!). Also, if you are vegetarian/vegan, just triple the vegetables to replace the chicken and cook for slightly longer to extract all the flavours.

YOU'LL NEED

1 tablespoon olive oil
4 onions, peeled and chopped into quarters
2 garlic bulbs, peeled and crushed
3 carrots, each chopped into thirds
3 stalks of celery, each chopped into thirds
1 whole chicken or chicken carcass
2 lemons
bunches fresh or dried herbs: parsley, chives, thyme, sage, whatever's on hand
+ salt and pepper, water

1. Into a big stock pot, pour some **olive oil** and add your **onions** for a few minutes to brown and caramelise (this is crucial!). Once the outsides are dark brown, then add your **garlic** and a dash more olive oil and get them cooking together for 1 minute.
2. Add your **carrot** and **celery** to the pot with the **chicken/carcass** and fill the pot up with **water** to just below the top. Juice the **lemons** and add to the pot along with the leftover lemon skins. Add **herbs** and a generous handful of **salt and pepper**. Put the lid on the pot and bring to the boil.
3. Once the pot has reached boiling, reduce heat and simmer for a minimum of 2 hours – the dream scenario being around 4 to 5 hours. If you've added a whole chicken, take it out after 1.5 hours and remove the meat (so it doesn't get overcooked). Then return the carcass to the stock mix for the remaining cook time.
4. Once finished cooking, remove the veggie bits from the stock and place it in the fridge (where it will last for three days) or in the freezer (for up to three months).

GRAZIE!

Firstly, Mum and Dad, you have been the constant beacon of grace, light, warmth and support in my life. I could not be more honoured to be half of two people. To my brother, Cameron, for always being my co-pilot in hard times. To my second parents, Israel and Edwina, for always keeping me safe in Melbourne – shalom.

The circle of friends who are family, if you know me as Jho, you know who you are. I can say with complete confidence and certainty that the world would not have P Mami, or this book, if you had not advocated for the real, chaotic me. You show up when everyone else runs away and for that, I'll love you all endlessly. The Sardinian castle is getting built for you all.

A huge and endless thank you to my Penguin Random House team of geniuses, more specifically to the special trifecta created between me, my publisher, and editor. Izzy, you so beautifully took, with enthusiasm and grace, my chaotic vision and turned it into a book that makes sense. Charle, you so perfectly gathered and tied the endless tales together while requesting me to dive deep and usher forth the best writer in me. To have found you both is a creative blessing and an example of patience for greatness. To Andy and Renee, for your brilliant and creative contribution.

To my P Mami community who come to my Pasta Clubs, buy my merch, cheer me on, support all my things, tell their friends . . . this one's for you! More notably, a thank you to a particular set of Plant Mama clients, the ones who trusted and believed in my creative craft when no one else did.

I am deeply thankful to a particular group of authors who have truly saved and grown me through their books. To the strangers who feel like sisters: Brené Brown, Elizabeth Gilbert, Glennon Doyle, Gabrielle Bernstein, Mel Robbins and of course, Oprah Winfrey. I will never take for granted the courage it takes to share what you think with the world in an effort to help others.

To the 14 kilos of brown and white fur currently sitting on my lap, Sprout. I am sane because of you and I'll repay you in bones and balls forever, my little Kouklitsa.

And finally, to me, JHo, as egotistical and immodest as it reads: writing this book was very hard and I pushed through during times when I did not think that it was possible to do so. You fucking did it! To little J in Year 7 who got her pen licence last, but now has her handwriting on the cover of her book: you are capable, sis. This is proof.

EBURY PRESS

UK | USA | Canada | Ireland | Australia
India | New Zealand | South Africa | China

Ebury Press is part of the Penguin Random House group of companies
whose addresses can be found at global.penguinrandomhouse.com

Penguin
Random House
Australia

First published by Ebury Press in 2023

Cover photography and illustrations by Jenna Holmes
Cover design by Andy Warren © Penguin Random House Australia Pty Ltd
Internal design by Andy Warren
Illustration on p. viii by Katie Ford. Additional photography credits: Barun Chatterjee (pp. 7, 104); *The Oprah Winfrey Show* (p. 18); Morgan Munday (pp. 19, 61, 88 top, 217); Benjamin Wright (p. 33); Frances Holmes (pp. 35 top left, 73 left, 117 left); Giovanna Gonzalez (p. 41); Laura Corfield (p. 42); Isabella Jacuzzi (pp. 69 bottom right, 77, 180 left, 182); Fred Rashid (p. 73 right); Georgia Snow (pp. 111, 117 right, 193 bottom); Kurt Falkenstein (p. 114); Odin Wilde (pp. 116, 127 top right, 136); Ruby Dennis (p. 119 top); Giuseppe Marano (p. 119 second from top); Ellie Coker (p. 119 third from top); Pip Newell (p. 126); Asti Alexander (pp. 132, 134); Erin Stebbins (p. 162); Erin Torgerson (p. 170); Nicole de Valter (p. 173 top right); Chelsea Allen (p. 205).
Typeset in 9.5/12 pt Abril Text by Post Pre-press Group, Australia

Printed and bound in China by 1010 Printing International

NATIONAL LIBRARY OF AUSTRALIA
A catalogue record for this book is available from the National Library of Australia

ISBN 978 1 76104 988 0

penguin.com.au

We at Penguin Random House Australia acknowledge that Aboriginal and Torres Strait Islander peoples are the Traditional Custodians and the first storytellers of the lands on which we live and work. We honour Aboriginal and Torres Strait Islander peoples' continuous connection to Country, waters, skies and communities. We celebrate Aboriginal and Torres Strait Islander stories, traditions and living cultures; and we pay our respects to Elders past and present.

PMAMI Manifesto

1. It is impossible to learn nothing from something

2. Follow with blind faith and focus on whatever makes you smile in the middle of a storm.

3. you have to actively be the sole architect in the creation of your pleasure home.

4. courage, creativity and character is a byproduct of knowing yourself.

5. Every connection has an intention, be it positive or negative.

6. When power is sent in a constructive & helpful direction - you can access your most aligned, regenerated & enthusiastic self.

7. The deeper reason of why you do something will determine the energy residing in the result.

8. The fastest route to an open mind and empathy is through the art of moving around. Do not waste the days in the same place.

9. You are protected when you are redirected.

PM